MODERN CANADIAN ESSAYS

Modern Canadian Essays

Edited by William H. New

Macmillan of Canada

ISBN 0-7705-1379-4

Printed in Canada for
The Macmillan Company of Canada Limited
70 Bond Street
Toronto, Ontario
M5B 1X3

Contents

Acknowledgements

"My Remarkable Uncle: A Personal Document" by Stephen Leacock is reprinted by permission of The Canadian Publishers, McClelland and Stewart Limited, Toronto.

"The Nature of Estuaries" from *Fisherman's Fall* by Roderick Haig-Brown is reprinted by permission of Collins Publishers, Toronto.

"On Racial Origins" from *Just Add Water and Stir* by Pierre Berton is reprinted by permission of The Canadian Publishers, McClelland and Stewart Limited, Toronto.

"Yat Hang Mew: The Best Damn Greengrocer You Ever Saw" first appeared in *Weekend Magazine*, May 24, 1975, and is reprinted by permission of Donald Cameron.

"Czechoslovakia" from *Home Country* by Peter C. Newman is reprinted by permission of The Canadian Publishers, McClelland and Stewart Limited, Toronto.

"When We Were Nearly Young" by Mavis Gallant, copyright © 1960 by The New Yorker Magazine Inc., is reprinted by permission of Georges Borchardt, Inc., 145 E. 52nd St., New York, N.Y.

"Encounter with an Archangel" from *The Rejection of Politics and Other Essays* by George Woodcock is reprinted by permission of New Press, Don Mills, Ontario.

"By Their Foods . . . " from *Scotchman's Return and Other Essays* by Hugh MacLennan is reprinted by permission of the Macmillan Company of Canada Limited.

"The Superiority of the Bilingual Brain" from *Second Thoughts: Science, the Arts, and the Spirit* by Wilder Penfield is reprinted by permission of The Canadian Publishers, McClelland and Stewart Limited, Toronto.

"The Word and the Place" from *Reality and Theatre* (original French edition, *Le Réel et le théâtral*) by Naim Kattan, translated by Alan Brown, is reprinted by permission of House of Anansi Press Limited.

"The Motive for Metaphor" from *The Educated Imagination* by Northrop Frye is reprinted by permission of Dr. H. Northrop Frye.

"The Windless World" from *Raisins and Almonds,* copyright © 1972 by Fredelle Bruser Maynard, is reprinted by permission of Doubleday and Co., Limited.

"Goldwin Smith" from *In Search of Canadian Liberalism* by Frank H. Underhill is reprinted by permission of the Macmillan Company of Canada Limited.

"Philosophy in the Mass Society" from *Philosophy in the Mass Age* by George Grant is reprinted by permission of Copp Clark Publishing.

"Doomsday Idealism" by Dave Godfrey from *Man Deserves Man,* edited by Bill McWhinney and Dave Godfrey, is reprinted by permission of McGraw-Hill Ryerson Limited.

"Genetics: Will This Science Save Us or Kill Us?" by David Suzuki first appeared in *Canada and the World,* Vol. 37 (February 1972), and is reprinted by permission of *Canada and the World.*

Introduction

THE ESSAY has long been a literary form in which writers engaged in debate, critical inquiry, and reflective comment. Their exchange of views established the intellectual milieu of their age, in which the arts either flourished or languished and the social fabric changed. In the twentieth century, and in Canada, as in any other place and time, this must be true. Yet it is also unlikely that one could ever successfully place restrictive national boundaries around any idea. The sixteen essays in this book must not, therefore, be considered an exhaustive representation of ''what Canadians think''; what they show is how some Canadian writers have responded to their own interests and experiences, and how, in developing ideas, they have given them particular form.

Hence the emphasis in this anthology is on diversity rather than on uniformity — a diversity of subject, style, tone, and structure. The subjects of the essays include culture and language, travel and education, history and politics, science and values. The styles range from the informal and journalistic to the formal and academic. The essays vary tonally, from the objective seriousness of David Suzuki's study of genetics to the passion of Dave Godfrey's political observations, and from the reflective ironies of Mavis Gallant's ''When We Were Nearly Young'' to the wit of Hugh MacLennan and Stephen Leacock. There are short essays and long essays, encompassing topics of different breadth and investigating them in varying degrees of depth. In Peter Newman's work, moreover, there is an example of how reorganization can affect an essay's impact. His several articles on Czech politics reached one audience when they were published separately in magazines; when he arranged them together under the general title "Czechoslovakia" in his book *Home Country*, they acquired a different tone, a kind of contrapuntal structure, and a cumulative meaning.

Whether an author's intent is to entertain, to instruct, or to convince his readers, he chooses a form that will best allow him to engage their attention. He may develop his argument deductively; he may use systems of classification and comparison; he may illustrate with a set of examples. He may blend various descriptive, narrative, and expository techniques and use humorous devices to serious ends. The balance, rather than the use of any single device, achieves his effect. Many of the writers in this anthology, for example, begin their essays with personal anecdotes. Some are amusing, some dispassionate. But this one particular form develops in a variety of ways and gives voice to many different attitudes and opinions.

If it is possible to see in this range of subjects and approaches certain of the preoccupations of Canadian life — responses to landscape, language, the survival of minority cultures, the processes of communication, and the implications of technology — it is also possible to read the essays for their intrinsic merits. Each author has handled his subject skilfully and demonstrated the art that makes good writing seem effortless.

MODERN CANADIAN ESSAYS

STEPHEN LEACOCK

My Remarkable Uncle:
A Personal Document

Try a char. sketch.

THE MOST REMARKABLE MAN I have ever known in my life was
my uncle Edward Philip Leacock—known to ever so many people
in Winnipeg fifty or sixty years ago as E.P. His character was so
exceptional that it needs nothing but plain narration. It was so
exaggerated already that you couldn't exaggerate it.

When I was a boy of six, my father brought us, a family flock, to
settle on an Ontario farm. We lived in an isolation unknown, in
these days of radio, anywhere in the world. We were thirty-five
miles from a railway. There were no newspapers. Nobody came
and went. There was nowhere to come and go. In the solitude of
the dark winter nights the stillness was that of eternity.

Into this isolation there broke, two years later, my dynamic Uncle
Edward, my father's younger brother. He had just come from a
year's travel around the Mediterranean. He must have been about
twenty-eight, but seemed a more than adult man, bronzed and
self-confident, with a square beard like a Plantagenet King. His
talk was of Algiers, of the African slave market; of the Golden
Horn and the Pyramids. To us it sounded like the *Arabian Nights*.
When we asked, "Uncle Edward, do you know the Prince of
Wales?" he answered, "Quite intimately" — with no further
explanation. It was an impressive trick he had.

In that year, 1878, there was a general election in Canada. E.P.
was in it up to the neck in less than no time. He picked up the

history and politics of Upper Canada in a day, and in a week knew everybody in the countryside. He spoke at every meeting, but his strong point was the personal contact of electioneering, of bar-room treats. This gave full scope for his marvellous talent for flattery and make-believe.

"Why, let me see" — he would say to some tattered country specimen beside him glass in hand — "surely, if your name is Framley, you must be a relation of my dear old friend General Sir Charles Framley of the Horse Artillery?" "Mebbe," the flattered specimen would answer. "I guess, mebbe; I ain't kept track very good of my folks in the old country." "Dear me! I must tell Sir Charles that I've seen you. He'll be so pleased." . . . In this way in a fortnight E.P. had conferred honours and distinctions on half the township of Georgina. They lived in a recaptured atmosphere of generals, admirals, and earls. Vote? How else could they vote than conservative, men of family like them?

It goes without saying that in politics, then and always, E.P. was on the conservative, the *aristocratic* side, but along with that was hail-fellow-well-met with the humblest. This was instinct. A democrat can't condescend. He's down already. But when a conservative stoops, he conquers.

The election, of course, was a walk-over. E.P. might have stayed to reap the fruits. But he knew better. Ontario at that day was too small a horizon. For these were the days of the hard times of Ontario farming, when mortgages fell like snowflakes, and farmers were sold up, or sold out, or went "to the States", or faded humbly underground.

But all the talk was of Manitoba now opening up. Nothing would do E.P. but that he and my father must go west. So we had a sale of our farm, with refreshments, old-time fashion, for the buyers. The poor, lean cattle and the broken machines fetched less than the price of the whisky. But E.P. laughed it all off, quoted that the star of the Empire glittered in the west, and off to the West they went, leaving us children behind at school.

They hit Winnipeg just on the rise of the boom, and E.P. came at once into his own and rode on the crest of the wave. There is something of magic appeal in the rush and movement of a "boom" town—a Winnipeg of the 80's, a Carson City of the 60's. . . . Life comes to a focus, it is all here and now, all *present,* no past and no outside—just a clatter of hammers and saws, rounds of drinks and rolls of money. In such an atmosphere every man seems a remarkable fellow, a man of exception; individuality separates out and character blossoms like a rose.

E.P. came into his own. In less than no time he was in everything and knew everybody, conferring titles and honours up and down Portage Avenue. In six months he had a great fortune, on paper; took a trip east and brought back a charming wife from Toronto; built a large house beside the river; filled it with pictures that he said were his ancestors, and carried on in it a roaring hospitality that never stopped.

His activities were wide. He was president of a bank (that never opened), head of a brewery (for brewing the Red River), and, above all, secretary-treasurer of the Winnipeg Hudson Bay and Arctic Ocean Railway that had a charter authorizing it to build a road to the Arctic Ocean, when it got ready. They had no track, but they printed stationery and passes, and in return E.P. received passes over all North America.

But naturally his main hold was politics. He was elected right away into the Manitoba Legislature. They would have made him Prime Minister but for the existence of the grand old man of the province, John Norquay. But even at that in a very short time Norquay ate out of E.P.'s hand, and E.P. led him on a string. I remember how they came down to Toronto, when I was a schoolboy, with an adherent group of "Westerners", all in heavy buffalo coats and bearded like Assyrians. E.P. paraded them on King Street like a returned explorer with savages.

Naturally E.P.'s politics remained conservative. But he pitched the note higher. Even the ancestors weren't good enough. He invented a Portuguese Dukedom (some one of our family once worked in Portugal) — and he conferred it, by some kind of reversion, on my elder brother Jim who had gone to Winnipeg to work in E.P.'s office. This enabled him to say to visitors in his big house, after looking at the ancestors — to say in a half-whisper behind his hand, "Strange to think that two deaths would make that boy a Portuguese Duke." But Jim never knew which two Portuguese to kill.

To aristocracy E.P. also added a touch of peculiar prestige by always being apparently just about to be called away—imperially. If some one said, "Will you be in Winnipeg all winter, Mr. Leacock?" he answered, "It will depend a good deal on what happens in West Africa." Just that; West Africa beat them.

Then came the crash of the Manitoba boom. Simple people, like my father, were wiped out in a day. Not so E.P. The crash just gave him a lift as the smash of a big wave lifts a strong swimmer. He just went right on. I believe that in reality he was left utterly bankrupt. But it made no difference. He used credit instead of cash. He still had his imaginary bank, and his railway to the Arctic Ocean. Hospitality still roared and the tradesmen still paid for it. Any one who called about a bill was told that E.P.'s movements were uncertain and would depend a good deal on what happened in Johannesburg. That held them another six months.

It was during this period that I used to see him when he made his periodic trips "east", to impress his creditors in the West. He floated, at first very easily, on hotel credit, borrowed loans and unpaid bills. A banker, especially a country town banker, was his natural mark and victim. He would tremble as E.P. came in, like a stockdove that sees a hawk. E.P.'s method was so simple; it was like showing a farmer peas under thimbles. As he entered the banker's side-office he would say: "I say. Do you fish? Surely that's a greenhart casting-rod on the wall?" (E.P. knew the names of everything.) In a few minutes the banker, flushed and pleased, was exhibiting the rod, and showing flies in a box out of a drawer. When E.P. went out he carried a hundred dollars with him. There was no security. The transaction was all over.

He dealt similarly with credit, with hotels, livery stables, and bills in shops. They all fell for his method. He bought with lavish generosity, never asking a price. He never suggested pay till just as an afterthought, just as he was going out. And then: "By the way, please let me have the account promptly. I may be going away," and in an aside to me, as if not meant for the shop, "Sir Henry Loch has cabled again from West Africa." And so out; they had never seen him before; nor since.

The proceeding with a hotel was different. A country hotel was, of course, easy, in fact too easy. E.P. would sometimes pay such a bill in cash, just as a sportsman won't shoot a sitting partridge. But a large hotel was another thing. E.P., on leaving—that is, when all ready to leave, coat, bag, and all — would call for his bill at the desk. At the sight of it he would break out into enthusiasm at the reasonableness of it. "Just think!" he would say in his "aside" to me, "compare that with the Hotel Crillon in Paris!" The hotel proprietor had no way of doing this; he just felt that he ran a cheap hotel. Then another "aside", "Do remind me to mention to Sir John how admirably we've been treated; he's coming here next week." "Sir John" was our Prime Minister and the hotel keeper hadn't known he was coming—and he wasn't. . . . Then came the final touch — "Now let me see . . . seventy-six dollars . . . seventy-six. . . . You give me"—and E.P. fixed his eye firmly on the hotel man — "give me twenty-four dollars, and then I can remember to send an even hundred." The man's hand trembled. But he gave it.

This does not mean that E.P. was in any sense a crook, in any degree dishonest. His bills to him were just "deferred pay", like the British debts to the United States. He never did, never contemplated, a crooked deal in his life. All his grand schemes were as open as sunlight — and as empty.

In all his interviews E.P. could fashion his talk to his audience. On one of his appearances I introduced him to a group of college friends, young men near to degrees, to whom degrees mean everything. In casual conversation E.P. turned to me and said, "Oh, by the way you'll be glad to know that I've just received my honorary degree from the Vatican—at last!" The "at last" was a knock-out — a degree from the Pope, and overdue at that!

Of course it could not last. Gradually credit crumbles. Faith weakens. Creditors grow hard, and friends turn their faces away. Gradually E.P. sank down. The death of his wife had left him a widower, a shuffling, half-shabby figure, familiar on the street, that would have been pathetic but for his indomitable self-belief, the illumination of his mind. Even at that, times grew hard with him. At length even the simple credit of the bar-rooms broke under him. I have been told by my brother Jim—the Portuguese Duke— of E.P. being put out of a Winnipeg bar, by an angry bar-tender who at last broke the mesmerism. E.P. had brought in a little group, spread up the fingers of one hand and said, "Mr. Leacock, five!" . . . The bar-tender broke into oaths. E.P. hooked a friend by the arm. "Come away," he said. "I'm afraid the poor fellow's crazy! But I hate to report him."

Presently even his power to travel came to an end. The railways found out at last that there wasn't any Arctic Ocean, and anyway the printer wouldn't print.

Just once again he managed to "come east". It was in June of 1891. I met him forging along King Street in Toronto — a trifle shabby but with a plug hat with a big band of crape round it. "Poor Sir John," he said. "I felt I simply must come down for his funeral." Then I remembered that the Prime Minister was dead, and realized that kindly sentiment had meant free transportation.

That was the last I ever saw of E.P. A little after that some one paid his fare back to England. He received, from some family trust, a little income of perhaps two pounds a week. On that he lived, with such dignity as might be, in a lost village in Worcestershire. He told the people of the village—so I learned later—that his stay was uncertain; it would depend a good deal on what happened in China. But nothing happened in China; there he stayed, years and years. There he might have finished out, but for a strange chance of fortune, a sort of poetic justice, that gave to E.P. an evening in the sunset.

It happened that in the part of England where our family belonged there was an ancient religious brotherhood, with a monastery and dilapidated estates that went back for centuries. E.P. descended on them, the brothers seeming to him an easy mark, as brothers indeed are. In the course of his pious "retreat", E.P. took a look into the brothers' finances, and his quick intelligence discovered an old claim against the British Government, large in amount and valid beyond a doubt.

In less than no time E.P. was at Westminster, representing the brothers. He knew exactly how to handle British officials; they were easier even than Ontario hotel keepers. All that is needed is hints of marvellous investment overseas. They never go there but they remember how they just missed Johannesburg or were just late on Persian oil. All E.P. needed was his Arctic Railway. "When you come out, I must take you over our railway. I really think that as soon as we reach the Coppermine River we must put the shares on here; it's too big for New York. . . . "

So E.P. got what he wanted. The British Government are so used to old claims that it would as soon pay as not. There are plenty left.

The brothers got a whole lot of money. In gratitude they invited E.P. to be their permanent manager; so there he was, lifted into ease and affluence. The years went easily by, among gardens, orchards, and fishponds old as the Crusades.

When I was lecturing in London in 1921 he wrote to me: "Do come down; I am too old now to travel; but any day you like I will send a chauffeur with a car and two lay-brothers to bring you down.'' I thought the "lay-brothers" a fine touch—just like E.P.

I couldn't go. I never saw him again. He ended out his days at the monastery, no cable calling him to West Africa. Years ago I used to think of E.P. as a sort of humbug, a source of humour. Looking back now I realize better the unbeatable quality of his spirit, the mark, we like to think just now, of the British race.

If there is a paradise, I am sure he will get in. He will say at the gate—"Peter? Then surely you must be a relative of Lord Peter of Tichfield?''

But if he fails, then, as the Spaniards say so fittingly, "May the earth lie light upon him.''

RODERICK HAIG-BROWN

The Nature of Estuaries

I REMEMBER THINKING, as a very small boy, that one of the supreme sights of the world must be the mouth of a river. I could not satisfactorily imagine this meeting of the river's flow and the sea's surge and I knew it would be a waste of time to ask anyone to describe it to me. Just what I expected I am not at all sure, but I suppose some sudden and violent outpouring of fresh water into salt, plainly visible, dramatic, and splendid. I knew little or nothing of tides and even less of the fearful things men do to river mouths in the process of civilization. So the first few estuaries I did finally see were disappointing and unconvincing.

Since that time I have seen many river mouths, large and small, and known many estuaries, spoiled and unspoiled. In general it is true that river mouths are not spectacular; one has to know and understand something of them to appreciate them. Even the youngest and wildest rivers tend to cushion their approach to immolation by building deltas of gravel and sand and mud. They slow down, wander into many channels, sharing these with the ebb and flow of the tides, and so meet the sea only in gradual transformation. It is interesting to remember that Captain George Vancouver, who made the first really thorough exploration of the Pacific Coast from California northward, failed to discover the mouths of the two largest rivers he passed, the Columbia and the Fraser. The Columbia, meeting the ocean majestically, disguises itself in the crashing white breakers that form and reform over its massive sand bars. The Fraser hides a dozen channels through mud and sand flats; Vancouver thought them navigable only by canoes. Farther up the coast he was disappointed again and again at the heads of the long inlets to find that they ended in "swampy low land" among the high mountains. Later, the first settlers built their homes near these low and swampy places, raised cattle on the slough hay and salt grasses and bred families of children who remembered the secrets of the tide flats all their lives.

This, then, is likely to be the way of estuaries. Only when one has walked the flat places and heard the wind in the grasses, explored the sloughs and side channels, watched the tides and faced the storms, does a river mouth take on character and substance and reveal its dramatic power. I know a few smaller streams that enter the sea directly, over falls or through rock-walled canyons, but even these are likely to have their flats of sand or gravel, revealed by the ebb of a long run-out, that time and flow will one day build higher.

Any estuary can be fished and most have fish somewhere about them — of all the angler's "likely places", few are more likely than where fresh and salt water meet and mingle. But the mouths of very large rivers are much like the sea itself; the river is lost in them and the fisherman becomes lost in them — he is fishing not an estuary but some little part of a great confusing reach of water. Even rivers of moderate size become very large where they meet the tides; too often one needs a boat and some very special local knowledge which leads to sloughs and side channels. Sometimes the main channel is exposed in pools and runs and riffles at low tide and there is nothing much better than this. But my preference is for the small streams and the creeks that one can manage — though often with difficulty—from one's feet and whose form and pattern is rarely altogether lost.

The sea trout of the Pacific Coast is the cutthroat. The rainbow runs to sea and becomes the steelhead, but he rarely lingers long in estuary waters. The Dolly Varden is also a sea-running fish, and in some estuaries he is fairly abundant, but he is not the equal of the cutthroat either as a fish or a fly-fisherman's fish. Cutthroats often run in good numbers to tiny creeks and may be found off them at certain tides and times. But the best cutthroat creeks are usually of fair size and, for some reason as yet unexplained, often have the amber-coloured water of the cedar swamps rather than clear flow of the mountains.

In this day of detailed research, surprisingly little is known of the cutthroat, especially in his sea-running phase. Life history, migration stages, feeding habits, stream preferences, all are matters of vague surmise and angler's observation. Even his peak spawning time remains a matter for debate, although it probably varies a good deal from one watershed to another. I know of no significant tagging program that has been carried out with migratory cutthroat, and I have only recently heard of a serious effort towards accurate scale reading.

In my experience, sea-running cutthroats rarely exceed four pounds, which suggests that they have a considerably more restricted migration than steelhead or salmon. They seem to spawn for the first time at fourteen or fifteen inches in length and a weight of about one and a half pounds; larger fish may be spawning for a second or third time. These larger fish seem to enter the rivers in July and August, well ahead of the main spawning run which comes in about the middle of November and is accompanied by good numbers of fish of about the same size that are not going to spawn. Spawning starts some time after Christmas and lasts until March, with a February peak in most streams. But there can be significant variations in both the timing and character of all these movements.

It is possible that cutthroats wander a considerable distance in salt water from their home rivers and they may enter other estuaries or streams to feed — there is nothing really to prove or disprove these theories, though precise knowledge would be important in management. But it is quite clear that some cutthroats are to be found in the estuaries of all but the smallest creeks in every month of the year. This is what makes them the main factor in estuary fishing; one may find other fish, but the cutthroats make it worthwhile to go fishing in the first place.

Tides play a big part in estuary fishing, but I must admit that after all these years I am never quite sure what it is. Fish do move in and upstream with the flood tide and they often feed well as they move. But they also feed well as they move downstream on the ebb. Both feeding and movement are generally better on large tides than on small ones, and I am quite sure that I have caught more estuary fish on the last two hours of a long ebb and the first hour of the flood than at any other stage. But I have also fished these stages a great deal more.

Estuaries, even of streams that are approximately the same size, differ enormously, and I think that common sense and personal preference, as well as those two fallibles, experience and local knowledge, should be allowed to enter into the choice of a fishing tide. Most of the small-stream estuaries I know fall into three main types. There are those which run out over shallow gravel bars, often dividing into several small channels; those which enter cleanly at high tide over a fall or a rocky bed and cut a long channel through sand or mud flats covered by salt water except on the lowest tides; and those that enter through salt-water meadows, cutting a long channel between high mudbanks. The first type is the most difficult and I suspect the least productive; the fish are usually scattered and one can only wade out hopefully with the last of the ebb and retreat gradually before the flood. At times, especially on the spring-fry run, the fish concentrate in the main channel as the flood comes well up in it, but one is usually backed into the brush by then and too close to them.

The second type is my favorite and is obviously most interesting to fish on a long ebb, when the flats are bare and the stream's channel across them is approachable and clearly defined. Such channels are often deeply cut and hold fish at all stages of tide, though it is logical to work out with the tide. On really low tides one can move right to the end of the channel and find fish feeding along the edge of the drop-off beyond it, then follow the tide back again as the flood starts up the channel. These streams usually have one or two well-defined tidal pools that can make sudden spells of good fishing towards the peak of the flood. But they are often disappointing and I rarely wait for that stage of the flood if I have found fish on the low tide.

The third type of estuary, where the stream has cut its channel through tidal meadows, is in many ways the most delightful of all. The low flatland gives a strong sense of space and freedom; every breeze over it is full of sound and meaning, changing the greens of weeds and grass in springtime, rattling the seed pods and dry stems of summer and fall. Mallard and pintails jump from sloughs and pot-holes, Wilson snipe flash from the grass knots and plunge down again into new hiding places; fall may bring a flock of snow geese or white fronts in migration. There is always life and movement somewhere on the flats and it has about it a special quality of wildness that belongs with salt spray and sea storms.

Where a river of fair size makes its way across such flats it is logical to fish the last of the ebb and the first of the flood. The main channel takes on the shape and character of its river; then one can move freely and the fish are more easily found. Often there are deepwater pools under the cut banks where some fish hold regardless of the retreating tide. There are riffles and runs and eddies, and plenty of current to help put life into the fly. But in the smaller streams none of this holds. When the channel is emptied of tide the stream's flow is too slight and shallow to hold fish. The few that are left behind are nervous and rarely feeding — one sees them by the ripple of their movement and knows the movement for flight or panic search for shelter. Intermediate tides are often favorable in these estuaries, though the last of the flood and the start of the ebb on big tides are likely to be most productive.

There is also a fourth type of stream to consider, so small that it has no real estuary at all and no clearly marked channel beyond its mouth. Many such streams breed considerable runs of both coho salmon and cutthroat trout, even though they may be so small that one can step across them in summer. As streams they are unfishable; one can poke a worm or a fly through the bush into some likely spot and perhaps hook a good fish but, profitable and demanding though this may be, interest in it tends to fade after one is ten or twelve years old and has learned to cast. The only real possibility is to meet the fish as they come to the creek's slight influence on a full-flood tide or find them as they hold and feed near the drop-off from its beach.

Either venture can be surprisingly successful when conditions are right. Finding the feeding fish at the drop-off is the less likely of the two and more demanding of precise local knowledge, but it yields a fine sense of achievement and very lively fishing. In the fall, usually in late September or October, both cohos and cutthroats will be holding off the creek, waiting for the rains to bring it up and let them in. Sometimes they take freely and well, more often they are scattered and uncertain, especially for the flyfisherman. But they are always worth a fly-fisherman's attention. Whether he can catch them or not, fish will be showing. He may grow weary with casting and curse the choice that limits his distance to fifty or sixty feet where the spinner is getting a hundred and fifty, but the very next cast and retrieve may get him a three-pound cutthroat or an old cock coho of ten or fifteen pounds. If he reflects for a moment he will remember that he has spent many weary hours on lakes far less attractive than his chosen creek mouth and without the slightest chance of such solid rewards as these.

These, then, are my estuaries, little places, often unconsidered, highly uncertain, pleasantly demanding of the skills a fisherman delights in. They are special places, ever changing with the tide's movements, full of the special life of the sea's meeting with the land. One grows to know them gradually, in rain and fog and sunshine, in wind and calm, at dawn and dusk; and as knowledge builds to intimacy the dramatic values are plain at last, richer and stronger than the simple splendor the child's mind hoped to discover.

PIERRE BERTON

On Racial Origins

MY FRIEND, Ray Silver, who is known in some quarters as "Lucky Silver" because during the war he survived three air crashes and a train wreck and was once hurled six hundred feet over a mountain into a different county, is having an argument with the Vital Statistics people.

It all began when, after the birth of his fourth baby, Lucky Silver got a government form asking him to name the racial origin of the parents.

Well, this made him both angry and confused. His maternal grandparents were born in the United States, his paternal grandfolk in the U.S.S.R. His maternal great-grandparents came from Alsace-Lorraine, which is either German or French, depending on the date. His paternal great-grandparents were from Poland. His wife's paternal line is Irish, but her maternal line is English and Cornish, and in addition there's a fair amount of Semitic strain in Silver from one side of the Urals or the other.

So, when Silver got this form asking him to state his new baby's racial origin he blew a gasket and wrote the following wonderful letter to the Deputy Registrar-General of the Government of Ontario:

DEAR MR. WALLACE: I am today in receipt of form 68(4)13-1691 over your signature requesting certain information in connection with the registration of a birth. Your records will show that I promptly complied with the provision of basic and pertinent data concerning the birth of our fourth child. However, I declined to state — or attempt to state — the racial origin of either my wife or myself. My reasons for so declining to comply are several, and are stated below:

I am aware that under the Vital Statistics Act you have the authority to prosecute and that I may be jailed, or fined, etc. Notwithstanding this threat to liberty of my person and property, let me state at the outset that I categorically refuse to provide any information whatsoever concerning "racial origin" of myself or any member of my family, at this or any future time. . . .

My peculiar reluctance to comply with a statement of racial origin on my own behalf or that of my family is influenced by:

1. The basis of your department for definition of such a term as "race" is absurdly unscientific and impossible to properly answer.

2. Racial statistics, so-called, have proven to be of little or doubtful significance and value to sociologists.

3. So-called racial data has too frequently been the material on which undemocratic procedures and philosophical bases for discrimination have been developed. The Rosenberg-Hegel philosophy of Nazi Germany, the racist policies of Strydom in South Africa, and the "mongrelization" theories of Southern Americans were all based on so-called racial distinction. I suggest—and am prepared to contest the conviction—that there is no place for such distinctions in the province of Ontario.

4. While I can trace one of my ancestors back to the person of a Russian prince who fought Gengis Khan, I have neither the time nor interest to pursue my other forbears back to a basic racial source. I am sure my wife would probably have as much difficulty in determining her origins.

> *I and my wife are native-born Canadians; my parents were both native-born Canadians.*

This may not satisfy your department, but I am sure it satisfies the purpose of any sociological pursuits which the Government of Ontario might reasonably be expected to pursue.

What Ray Silver is saying is that he is a mammal, and that is as far as he is prepared to go, and that anybody who takes up time trying to trace his racial origin through his father's father's father's father would be better employed making party pics out of old toothbrush handles.

For this system, which insists that your "racial origin" is determined by the country your father comes from, makes no sense at all.

If your father comes from Armenia they put you down as an Armenian in origin, even if *his* father was a Zulu. Yet, if your father comes from Canada you are not allowed to put your racial origin down as Canadian because, they tell you patiently, the word "Canadian" doesn't identify you by race. And that's quite right; but neither does the word "English", for most Englishmen are a bastard mixture of Celtic, Roman, Saxon, Danish, and Norman.

I feel keenly about this because it so happens that my family has been on this side of the Atlantic since the year 1681. Before that they came from France and from Germany and from England and from God knows where.

What, then, is my racial origin? I say it is Canadian, if we are going to use terms loosely. But why use terms like "racial origin" at all when they are so inexact?

The statistics that these forms reveal are, quite obviously, misleading and dishonest. After eleven generations am I still a Frenchman, rather than a North American? Are my children, who are half Scottish, to be listed as French because three hundred years ago one of my ancestors was a Huguenot?

The Ontario government quite rightly no longer allows any employer to inquire about his prospective employees' racial background since, under the Fair Employment Practices Code, such information is held to be irrelevant.

It is not only irrelevant, it is meaningless. And it is more than meaningless: it is dangerous since its official acceptance contrives to prop up the silly arguments of the racial purists.

There is no such thing as racial purity, of course, and in this great melting pot of a country we ought long since to have stopped pretending on our official forms that there is.

PS There has been no official reply to Lucky Silver's letter. Perhaps up at Queen's Park they are hoping that if everybody forgets about it, the nasty problem will go away.

DONALD CAMERON

Yat Hang Mew: The Best Damn Greengrocer You Ever Saw

HIS ACTUAL NAME, it appears, is Yat Hang Mew, but everyone knew him as Angus. He is one of those shadowy figures one remembers from childhood with diffuse affection: always present, always smiling, assuring a child by his mere presence that familiar things were in their familiar places. Angus was the proprietor of Varsity Produce, a greengrocer's shop at 10th and Sasamat, in the university district of Vancouver.

Angus, genuinely, has a place among my earliest memories. We moved to Vancouver in 1939, when I was two, and soon Angus had anchored himself firmly in our lives. My mother would lift the phone and give the number, and when Angus answered she would tell him what she wanted. Then she would ask him whether he had any "unusual commodities" and if he had, say, fresh asparagus, she would order that.

An hour or two later Angus would clatter down the street in his truck, an old Dodge pickup the color of well-laundered blue jeans, with a high canopy like an open carport built up over the box. Up the steps he would come, his box laden with tomatoes and cabbage, apples and asparagus. He'd smile and chat a moment, then he'd be off again, idling down the street to the next customer.

I somehow thought of him as an old man—but then when you're three or four everyone over ten seems venerable. Those days are now distant and sunlit as a mirage, those days before dial telephones and automatic transmissions, when a young professor and his wife could hire a maid for $17 a month and her keep.

Years pass, things change, boys grow up. I walked off the big
jetliner from Montreal this spring into a cloud of immigrants from
Asia, Indians mostly, for Vancouver is—as Vancouverites somewhat uneasily boast — Canada's gateway to the Orient. Black
skins, brown, white, and yellow; turbans, saris, business suits,
and Pentax cameras; a jangle of languages, and English spoken to
the lilts of a dozen other cultures; a rich potpourri of humanity
swirling around my petite, white-haired mother. We drove down-
town, I installed myself on the 17th floor of a hotel tower, and
Mother said I should look up Angus.

"Angus! Is he still alive?"

"He certainly is," said Mother. "He sold the Varsity Produce
several years ago, and now he's in real estate. He's doing very
well. I'm sure he'd love to see you."

I found Angus in a spacious yellow stuccoed house on a broad,
well-tended lot about a block from the site of his old shop. He met
me at the door, dapper in a three-piece suit, a Chinese newspaper
in his hand—a cheerful, confident man who has been touched very
lightly by the 35 summers which have flown since we met. He
ushered me into a comfortable living room, settled himself in a
chair among the poinsettias, fan palms, and philodendrons, inquired about my mother, and told me something of his life.

How little we know of the people around us! What extraordinary
quests and trials, what despairs and ecstasies are hidden behind the
eyes we meet casually on the bus, at the beach, over the counter!
And history: how we are all the playthings of history, of chance
and mythology.

Angus was born in Shekki, in the Pearl River district of
Kwangtung Province, about 80 miles from Hong Kong. He was
one of ten children, and his older brother, Yat Kai Mew, had
migrated to Canada. At 15, Hat Hang Mew followed him. But his
brother, ten years older, couldn't sponsor him; the federal government had just passed an immigration act which had the effect of
cutting off Chinese immigration into Canada. Between 1911 and
1922, roughly 2,300 Chinese a year had entered Canada. During
the next 23 years a grand total of eight were admitted. The only
exceptions were merchants, consuls, and students—and so it was

that Yat Hang Mew entered Canada as a student, the son of Jung Won Leung.

He enrolled in Strathcona School, in a class almost entirely Chinese. "I wanted to learn English, you know?" he grins, speaking half a century later with a touch still of Chinese accent. "So I took the first seat in the first row, right up front. I didn't want to miss *anything*. Our teacher, Miss Coleman, she spoke a little bit of Chinese. Her father was a missionary in China, and he *really* spoke Chinese, but she didn't pronounce it well—it's hard, a hard language. We had a lot of fun with her pronunciation.

"Well, after a couple of weeks she said, that's enough fooling around, we have to get down to work. I'm going to put a list of English names on the board, and I want each of you to pick one, then you'll have a name English people can remember. So she put the list on the blackboard, and I thought, I'm in the first seat in the first row, so I'll take the first name. Which was 'Angus'. The names were all the same to me, you know. But it was a good choice. Wherever I went, people remembered 'Angus'.

"Then I had a choice, which high school to go to. I could have gone to King Ed, where there were lots of our people, but I chose Kitsilano. I was the only Chinese student in the school, and that's why I went. The only way to learn a language is to plunge right in. You have to answer questions, explain yourself, understand everything — all in English."

Angus had a friend, Kee Gee, who ran a farm in Coquitlam, and who hadn't mastered English very well. "He would get advice from the Canadian farmers," Angus remembers, "and he couldn't understand what they were telling him. So I used to interpret for him. Then a bit later he bought the Varsity Produce, and put my name in as his partner, even though I was in China at the time. He's a wonderful man, just a wonderful man; we were partners 37 years and we never had a quarrel. . . ."

Wait a minute, now. You were in *China*?

"Oh yes. We used to go back to China every four or five years." He laughs. "Most people take vacations a couple of weeks a year, but we went for a whole year, and the other partner took care of the

shop.'' He laughs again. ''We had a good business, we made lots
of money. If I'd invested it all I'd be a millionaire today. But we
spent it travelling back and forth by ship to China, you see? We
were really working for the CPR.''

For 25 years, in fact, Angus had two lives. In China he married,
acquired property, and fathered three children. In Canada he ran
the Varsity Produce, invested what he could, and waited patiently
for the immigration laws to be eased. If he had wanted to, Angus
would have been hard-pressed to find a Chinese bride in Canada;
as James Morton points out in his recent book, *In the Sea of Sterile
Mountains: The Chinese in British Columbia,* the 1941 census
showed more than 16,000 Chinese men in the province, and only
2,400 women — a result, presumably, of British Columbia's
virulent anti-Orientalism. Men might be permitted in to do jobs
white men disdained, but we were not about to encourage them to
bring their wives and settle.

Morton's book is painful reading. Here is Premier S. F. Tolmie
sternly warning that ''the country and its representatives had better
wake up if we are to preserve Canada as a white man's country.''
Here is Fred Hume, later mayor of both New Westminster and
Vancouver, seconding a motion in favor of complete exclusion of
Oriental immigrants. Here is A. M. Manson, attorney-general and
later a Supreme Court justice, declaring that ''We want British
Columbia to be a white man's country.'' Here are women's
groups, early socialists, the board of trade, the Farmers' Institute,
and the British Columbia Federation of Labor all clamoring
against the Chinese.

Worst of all, here is the Asiatic Exclusion League meeting in
1907, being addressed by a Presbyterian minister, the Rev. Dr.
H. W. Fraser, who claims that if the influx is not stopped at once,
his own pulpit will soon be in the hands of ''a Jap or a Chinaman''.
Thirty thousand people listened to such tripe, spoken from the
steps of the city hall, on the very edge of the Chinese quarter. Not
surprisingly, a mob that night rampaged through Chinatown,
smashing windows and beating Chinese people while families
cowered in their barricaded stores.

That was the year Angus was born. By the time he got to Canada, things were a little better, but as late as 1935, when he was well-established in business, a full-page ad for the Liberal Party said, in part, that "A vote for any CCF candidate is a vote to give the Chinaman and Japanese the same voting right that you have! A vote for a Liberal candidate is a vote against Oriental enfranchisement."

As Angus says, "We were then where the East Indians are today." Even the occupations open to a Chinese were severely limited. "We were good farmers," Angus smiles, "so we were allowed to farm. We were good cooks, so we could operate restaurants. We could run laundries or small food stores, we could work in the lumber mills, just the same way the black people were allowed to be porters and work on the railways. That was all that was allowed."

So Angus and Kee Gee made themselves into the best damn greengrocers you ever saw. At 4 or 5 in the morning Kee Gee would take the other truck, the big international, down to Chinatown, where the market gardeners from South Vancouver and the Fraser Delta would have the produce stacked in boxes along the curb. "To get something scarce, something unusual, you had to be there early, you see?" explains Angus. I wish I had seen it: the Chinese farmers, the owners of little groceries all over town, the trucks creeping along in the darkness while the boxes were put off and on, the haggling in the singing dialects of China, the greetings, the jokes, the money changing hands. "All gone now," Angus shrugs. "Old-fashioned. Now the farmers sell direct to the wholesale departments of the chain stores." In its day, though, the Keefer Street market must have been like Covent Garden conducted in Chinese, in the heart of a city I once considered bland.

"The whole secret of our business was estimating," Angus declares. "We had to estimate exactly how much we'd need of each kind of produce, how much we could sell that day — you know, not to run short, but not to be left with produce that would go bad. Everything we dealt with was perishable — fruit, vegetables, flowers. You had to estimate exactly.

"Every day of the year was different. Different things in season, different volume of business. December 24th, Christmas Eve, that was the busiest day of the whole year. The shop would be jammed in the morning, and we'd rush, rush all day — and by the evening there wouldn't be a thing left except maybe one bunch of flowers, and somebody would hurry in and say, Yes, that's just what I want!"

In the early days, Kee Gee and some of the employees had trouble remembering the names of their customers, though they could remember the addresses. "I got an extra Point Grey phone book," Angus chuckles. "It wasn't very big then, not that many people had phones. I cut it all up and re-arranged it by street and house number, so you could say, 4510 West 7th — OK, that's Mrs. So-and-so. People were really surprised that we always knew the names, even if we were only there once." He giggles. "I never told them about that phone book."

Angus insisted that Varsity Produce offer personal service: "You had to know that with this person the back door was open, and you were supposed to go in, put the vegetables in the icebox, the fruit in the bowl on the table, and she'd leave a vase out for the flowers. Or if a lady came along and said she was having a party Saturday night and she wanted to serve avocados, then I knew I had to get them Tuesday and ripen them in the warm room — not too fast, or I'd cook them and they'd be like rubber. You see? You can buy them green, but you can't serve them that way, they're worth nothing."

Halfway across the world, the armies of Japan were marching into China. Angus's wife tried to protect the three children, tried to ensure they were fed and sheltered, even if it meant becoming rundown and undernourished herself. Eventually she contracted tuberculosis, and when Canada's immigration laws were finally relaxed in 1947 to permit the entry of wives and unmarried children, Ng Wai Lueng was still barred by her health. She died in 1952, and Angus brought the children to Vancouver.

A light suddenly broke over me.

"Angus," I said, "when I was in high school a fellow named

Jock Leung came into our class in the middle of the year. He was straight from China, and he could hardly speak any English at all. . . . ''

"Jock, yes," grinned Angus. "My oldest son." He points to a framed graduation portrait. "That's him there, he's a doctor now."

Imagine that: I remember it vividly, this kid a bit older than the rest of us, and everyone wanting to be friendly and make him feel at home, but stymied and embarrassed by the language gap. I remember we smiled a lot, and he smiled back.

"Bright guy," I said, studying the picture for some trace of the shy, friendly boy who joined our class all those years ago.

"He gets that from his mother," Angus nodded. "When I went back to China, I used to spend my time studying Chinese language and literature. I remember my wife saying, Come to bed! It's late! and I would say, No, I have to repeat this essay for my teacher tomorrow — that's the way they taught, you see, you had to memorize a whole essay at a time.

"Well, you're pretty dumb if you can't do that, my wife would say, and she'd repeat the whole thing off, lying there in bed. I hadn't learned it, but she'd learned the whole essay just from hearing me repeat it over and over. Jock has that from her. So has my daughter Florence, in the other picture, she's a nurse. My second son, Norman, he's dead."

Angus was silent for a little while.

In 1956 Angus went back to Hong Kong and married his second wife, Anne. They have four children, three girls and a boy, and the youngest, Winston, is the same age as my eldest. Which says something amusing about my assumption years ago, that Angus was an old man. He's only 67 now, in fact.

How did he get into real estate?

"I told you about my partner, what a fine man he is, and how he trusted me. I was the privileged one, you know, I dealt with the customers, did all the banking, all the paying, kept the books. At the end of the year, I would give him a paper, saying this is what we took in, this is what we spent, here's the profit, and here's your half — I'd give him the money.

"But he'd take the paper, and he'd do this!" Angus crumpled up a sheet of paper. "And he'd throw it in the stove! I'd say, hey, don't do that, I can't get you another. But he'd say, I got my money, what do I need a paper for?

"Well, we had a customer on 10th, just where the Bank of Montreal is now, a very nice lady. I used to take her groceries over and sometimes I'd have a cup of coffee with her and talk for a few minutes at the end of the day. I'd be gone from the shop, but my partner would never say anything about it. One night, I was just coming from her place and I saw a For Sale sign going up on a building across the street. We'd been looking for some property to invest in, so we bought that one, and that was the beginning of it."

Now Angus owns, he says, "a few pieces of property". Rumor has it that he actually owns several considerable pieces of income property in the premium shopping area just outside the university gates.

By the mid-1960s, things had changed. Where Angus once lived above the shop, sending money to his family in China, he now lived with his second family in the big house round the corner. The Chinese community not only had the vote, but had even sent a member to Parliament. Chinese-Canadians were prominent in medicine, dentistry, and the law; no longer hived up in Chinatown, Chinese families were spread throughout the city.

People like Angus, however, remained in an oddly precarious position. Well-established though they might be, they were still illegal immigrants, subject to deportation. One of the darker results was blackmail. "When someone found out your name was not what you said it was," Angus remarks, "they would threaten you: pay me so much or I turn you in. Lots of people paid, but I didn't. I said, I'd rather go back to China, and have *you* in jail for extortion."

Ultimately the federal government offered illegal immigrants a chance to normalize their status — and, after some hesitation, Angus did so. "The immigration officer was suspicious," he recalls. "He said, why did you take so long? Who are you protecting? Well, of course, I wasn't protecting anyone, the person who arranged the papers for me to come to Canada was dead by then,

,but I told him I had a business as Angus Leung, and children to think about, and it wasn't easy to go back to my true name. When I told the immigration man that, he understood.''

Angus was thinking about giving up his business, too.

"The way we did business was outa date, outa date. You can get anything in Safeway now — when we started you couldn't, but now you can. The bank had been after our property for years, and West Point Grey was growing so fast, a little grocery store couldn't stand in the way of progress. And my children were in school, but I never saw them, I was in the shop till 10, 10:30 at night. My wife said, Angus, they need you; I can't speak enough English to help them with their schoolwork.''

In 1968, Angus sold the Varsity Produce. He had been doing business at 10th and Sasamat for 37 years. He thought he had retired — but then his friends began asking him for advice about real estate. He had good connections in the Chinese community, he was known as a shrewd investor, and before long he had a realtor's licence and an arrangement with Sasamat Realty. Last year he more or less became inactive, though he still makes a deal or two when one comes along. Now he devotes his time to his family, his friends, his fellows in the West Point Grey United Church.

"Westerners," he says, "are ahead of the Chinese in technology, no question about that. But we are way ahead in family life, in friendship.''

Nobody who surveys the wreckage of modern Canadian family life can possibly deny it. There is something to be learned from Angus, from his cheerful perseverance in the face of prejudice and restriction, from the balance with which his living room remains Canadian, and yet is subtly transformed by the artistry and values of a civilization which was old when Socrates began teaching in the little town of Athens.

Vancouver as a whole is perhaps beginning to achieve a little of that balance. Anyone can see the relationship between Montreal and Paris, between Halifax and London; the flavor of Vancouver, by contrast, is considerably Asian, from the restaurants and import shops to the Nitobe Gardens and the Asian Studies program at UBC, from the Sikh temples to the Japanese officers of the fishermen's union, from the Roberts Bank superport which ships coal to Japan to the little groceries across the city which are invariably run by the Chinese.

"Racial discrimination," declared Alan Morley in *Vancouver, From Milltown to Metropolis* (1969), "is a thing of the past in Vancouver." At the time it must have seemed so; today, with the influx from Hong Kong and India over the past few years, racism is again rearing its distorted features in the city. It is hardly surprising: with a vacancy rate of less than one per cent in housing, and some elementary school classes in which only three children of 40 speak English, the city's systems are under considerable strain. "In another generation," a Vancouverite muttered to me ominously, "our children are going to be working for these people." Perhaps — and why not? If you have to have a boss, what difference does it make that his skin is yellow, or brown, or candy-striped? If I had to work again for wages, I would be grateful for an employer of Angus's wit, cheerfulness, and humanity.

Canadians are debating immigration policy these days with a vigor we have not seen for years, and immigration is a long-term investment. It hurts at the time, and the benefits flow only in the distant future. But we could do worse than to remember Angus, the corner grocer who carved such a niche for himself in the life of West Point Grey, who nourished our avocados while his family waited patiently in China. We did our best to keep him out. If we had succeeded, we would have been much the poorer.

PETER NEWMAN

Czechoslovakia

I WAS GOING BACK to Czechoslovakia this summer, after thirty
years, to visit Prague and a little border town called Breclav, where
my father was once the president of an industrial complex and I
was a much-protected and happy little boy. I had been thinking of
it as that most sentimental of journeys, the native's return, and had
hoped to indulge myself in spirit and in print in a reprise of a whole
life style that had been kept alive in my memory by my relatives
who loved their country, Czechoslovakia, as fiercely as I love my
own, Canada.

When I saw Prague last it was March, 1939, that sad winter after
Munich, and the tanks the Czechs were gazing at were German
tanks. We had stayed far too long, months after many of my
parents' friends had fled the country. But my father, Oskar Newman, was a politically active nationalist, an economic adviser to
the Benes government, "a true Czech", as such men were called
to differentiate them from the Sudetenland Germans. He was filled
with a naïve optimism that, despite everything, the Western al-
liance would not let the Czechs down and it was only the fact that
his wife and child were candidates for Nazi concentration camps
that persuaded him to leave at all. To him, and to the thousands of
Czech patriots like him who saw their young country as a bastion
of freedom in Central Europe, the Munich pact of 1938 between
the English, the French, the Italian, and the Germans was a
betrayal of the human spirit. Still, he believed that the agreement,

under which Czechoslovakia gave up its fortified frontiers for the sake of "peace in our time", would sate the Germans' lust for *Lebensraum*.

Even though we lived in the Sudetenland, we stayed on. At the end of September, after being bombed, we left the Breclav house, which the Nazis soon occupied and turned into a gambling casino, and took refuge with my grandparents in the capital. So I was in Prague on the morning of March 15, 1939, and saw through excited nine-year-old eyes the panzer troops pouring into the city, heralded by bombers. Motorcycles, gun carriers, tanks, armoured cars with ice on their running-boards, roared through the misty morning. The first soldiers were young and nervous, fodder for the resisting guns that were never fired; then came the veteran officers, in shiny Mercedes, and, like crows of ill-omen, the black-uniformed Gestapo.

Prague was full of strangers that day. Trade fairs the week before had been infiltrated by hundreds of Germans who now lined the streets, cheering, to give newsreel cameramen the impression that Czechs were welcoming the invasion. Three thousand German students had enrolled the year before in Prague universities, and now they had uniforms on and were marshalling the crowds. Czechs walked by the tanks with averted eyes; civil disobedience was not a creed then, and the Czech army, denied its fortifications, had crumbled without a fight. In the marketplace, women sat amidst the stalls of goose-liver pâtés and fresh sweet butter, crying.

We were all outfitted with gas masks in long grey canisters that were made in Japan, didn't work, and looked like Hallowe'en toys. The stores were selling flashlights with blue glass for the blackouts. The affluent were trying desperately to convert money into negotiable assets. (My father bought sheets of valuable stamps which I was supposed to smuggle out of the country in the guise of a child's stamp collection. But I traded them off to another boy for a cap pistol to shoot Germans. When my father discovered this as we crossed the border on falsified passports, he was too anguished even to care.)

The newspapers were still free that one final day (and until the last few months, for only one three-year period in thirty years have they ever been free again) and published black-bordered editions. There were a thousand rumours. The Germans were supposed to be confiscating onions by the kilo to make poison gas. It was a measure of our innocence that nothing more horrible than World War I style gassings was imaginable. Ambulances screamed across the city and were said wryly to be carrying German officers sick on whipped-cream cakes from the coffee shops. Jews were committing suicide. All was lost in twenty-four hours.

It was a sad capitulation, not in the country's tradition. Czechoslovakia had been united only two decades earlier out of a nervous conglomeration of Germans, Moravians, Slovaks, and Rusyns added to the Bohemian heartland. The various nations that formed the new Czechoslovakia had been sturdily resisting oppression for a thousand years. But it was the Czech's geographical misfortune to block the path to Russia and the Balkans from easy access by the Germans, who were ever mindful of Bismarck's dictum: "Whoever controls Bohemia, controls Europe."

The character of the Czech people has always had two strains. As a beachhead of Western culture in Eastern Europe, they are imbued with both the Western tradition of liberal humanism and with a Slavic fatalism which allows small men to make prudent adjustments to overwhelming realities.

The Czech ambiance is far more difficult to capture than that of the flamboyant European races — the French, the Italians, the Hungarians. But there was something of its grace exhibited at Expo in 1967 and it was caught beautifully in the prize-winning film *Closely Watched Trains,* in which the anti-hero, the young trainman, gives up his life in resistance to the Nazis but as a throwaway gesture, bravely but unemotionally — dying absurdly in the midst of full life. The Czechs are courageous but careful. De-Stalinization was begun in the country only in 1963, seven years after Khrushchev's anti-Stalin speech had cleared the way for the Hungarian uprising of 1956.

Young Czechs may have found the fumes of freedom heady this

year, but Alexander Dubcek himself never intended to launch a revolution. Men of his generation are by nature unwilling to go too far because they know that their country has been betrayed three times before by the free West—in 1938 at Munich; in 1945, when the Americans allowed Russia to occupy Prague; and in 1948, when the world watched the Communist takeover in February.

It is a bad joke among Czechs that Western statesmen are forever saying, "Of course we sympathize with you, but we can't do anything." Even in this context, Mitchell Sharp's initial lukewarm response to the Russian invasion as being "disappointing" or maybe even "regrettable" seemed a hell of a way to write off the freedom of a people.

Still, no words, however stirring, will help the Czechs now and those among them with long memories must be saying again, as the paper *Lidove Novidny* did in its lead article on the day of the Nazi invasion so long ago: "We wanted to sing with the angels but now we must howl with the wolves." [1968]

II

SPRING STEALS RELUCTANTLY into this ancient, threadbare but still bewitchingly beautiful city without stirring the hopes that usually mark the end of winter. This is Prague two years after the Czechs reached out for freedom with an impulse that spread like bushfire, only to be extinguished by the Russian invasion of 1968. The interval has been a time without seasons, a sad span of endurance with a scarcely bearable present and no obvious future.

The Czechs have little left to sustain them now except the characteristic black humour that has always baffled their invaders. "Which country has the highest mountains in the world?" a taxi driver will ask over his shoulder, and then answer ruefully, through the side of his mouth: "Czechoslovakia. After all, we've been going downhill for thirty years." A man in a beer hall will lean over and recount a favourite aphorism: "There really are only two ways left to get rid of the Russians: the natural way, with the Angel Michael descending from heaven to drive them out with his flaming sword, or the supernatural way, with the Supreme Soviet ordering them to climb back into their tanks and toddle off home.''

This kind of wit springs from a depth of political cynicism so remote from the North American experience that it is almost impossible to grasp. Detachment from one's environment can strengthen the human spirit only if it is based on some timeless conviction, and the Czechs are fortifying their souls with the belief that their little country, which managed to survive three centuries of Hapsburg despotism and six years of Nazi occupation, can outlast the Russian empire as well. ''We are not born to be governed easily,'' they boast, asserting their national destiny through inner rebellion, like existential heroes in a novel by Camus. The Czechs' determination to outlive and, if possible, to outwit the Russians bears little relationship to the situation as it exists.

The dismemberment of Alexander Dubcek's brave dreams of a humane communism is almost complete — censorship has been reimposed, the borders have been resealed, and there are constant rumours of mass arrests and possible show trials.

At the moment, there is a struggle for power within the first circle of the Czech Communist party and the very real fear of a purge in party ranks. All 1,600,000 members of the party — out of a total population of about 14,500,000 — have had to turn in their red cloth cards. Only those deemed sufficiently loyal to the Soviet Union (or able to prove they were ''misled'' by ''Dubcek's counter-revolutionary tendencies'') will be reinstated. Having a party card can mean the difference between being able to practise your profession or being forced into manual labour, educating your children or sending them into factories, getting a new apartment or sharing a single room.

These and other punitive measures would seem to indicate a final Russian triumph over Czech liberalism. But in Czechslovakia these days, truth is not always the sum of the ascertainable facts. Having tasted liberty, the Czechs have become aware of the difference between freedom and power. Having tried and failed to make their brand of communism more progressive, they are set on a carefully contrived course of passive resistance which could, in the long run, prove more effective than their short-lived revolt. Their natural effervescence long gone, the Czechs are instinctively functioning as a silent, passive majority by deliberately opting out of political involvement. This "internal migration" is evident among workers, students, and intellectuals alike and amounts to a nationwide lethargy that threatens to ruin an already fragile economy.

It is a tactic without leadership but not without cunning, based on the theory that only by returning some of the freedoms withdrawn since August, 1968, will the Czechoslovak government be able to ensure the kind of economic performance from their people being demanded by the Russians. The Czech version of passive resistance takes many subtle forms and can be seen in the faces of hundreds of people all over Prague — in the swift passage of a smile curving the lips of a postman as he watches two Russian officers trying to find their way through a maze of narrow alleyways, in the mechanical tone of an official government spokesman, parroting the party line while his hands drum lightly on a table top, sending out a wordless message as if to say, "Don't pay too much attention to this canned crap. After all, I do not control the mysteries of life. I am only part of them, and all the world knows the truth about the Russians."

The longer Prague remains an occupied city, the more this spirit of silent rebellion grows. Most of the seventy thousand Russians still stationed on Czech soil stay out of sight in armouries and suburban barracks. But occasionally, and always in pairs, Russian officers can be seen, briefcases firmly in hand, stomping through the streets or standing in the lobby of the Hotel Yalta. A midnight ride through the deserted city shows that the only building surrounded by policemen with glistening sub-machine-guns is the headquarters of the Czechoslovak-Soviet Friendship Society. "We have to guard it because people are always trying to throw bricks through the windows," a Czech policeman explains, with grave decorum and dancing eyes.

It is somehow incongruous that this drama of human repression and resentment should be happening in Prague, which is still, quite simply, the most beautiful city in the world. The magnificent sweep of Hradcany Castle dominates the skyline, managing to combine the best of Romanesque, Gothic, renaissance, and baroque architecture, the gleaming spires of St. George's Basilica (which have been looking down on Prague since 1142), the ancient Charles Bridge, whose sculptured supports slope down to the whispering weirs of the Moldau — all these and the city's many other wonders now seem museumlike, detached from the harsh realities of the moment.

The light comes to Prague these spring mornings as it might come into the boudoir of a once very beautiful, now very old, woman, living on memories and gallantry. Spontaneous gaiety is so rare that when it happens, passers-by stop and stare — at dogs frolicking in a churchyard, at a student, handsome in an ancient fur hat, making jokes about a group of East German tourists standing stolidly to watch the statues of saints emerge out of the old town-hall clock as it strikes the hour. There is little traffic except for taxis, aged coal trucks, and the black, chauffeur-driven Tatras owned almost exclusively by party functionaries. The cars' rapacious snouts make them look like schools of sharks as they cruise the streets between government ministries.

It is a city of wild contrasts. The tourist hotels smell of sweat and old pork fat, but they serve drinks in exquisite Czech crystal glasses. Office workers eat, in the buffets of Wenceslas Square, hors d'oeuvres made of goose-liver pâté or caviar frosted with swirls of mayonnaise, while standing upright at plastic-topped tables in fifteen-year-old overcoats.

People find their only emotional outlet in the city's cultural life. Prague has five symphony orchestras and twenty-eight theatres, most playing every week night. This month alone it is possible to see performances of plays by Shakespeare, Anouilh, Christopher Fry, Edward Albee, and Peter Ustinov, operas by Smetana, Tchaikovsky, Strauss, and Bizet as well as ballets, pantomimes, and art exhibitions. At one concert, which featured the Prague symphony playing Vivaldi's *Four Seasons* with a young Czech violinist as soloist, the vivacity of the crowd was astonishing. Everyone looked shabby — to be anything else is an affront to humanity in Prague—but almost everybody was full of the kind of joyful anticipation you see in North America only on the faces of five-year-olds watching a magician. People were there for a good time, and they found not just pleasure in the music but hope—and for some the hopefulness was too much. By the end of the performance, their faces were wet with tears. [1970]

III

HE LOOKED SOMEHOW LIKE A CAPTIVE CHIPMUNK—shrewd, with darting eyes, clawing at a world he had helped to make and now wanted to destroy. One of the middle-aged journalists who had supported Alexander Dubcek's liberalization in 1968, he had been forced out of his profession. But I had been told where to find him, and now he was expressing some of the thoughts he could no longer publish himself.

We met at the back of a large beer hall in Prague's Old Town. During an hour's conversation he sat hugging himself, as though the warmth of the tavern were some precious contraband that could be smuggled out, hoarded against the cold March wind rattling the windows. At the beginning, our conversation was halting, as stylized as a burlesque routine — a systematic progression of disclosures, with the journalist guarding against spontaneous reactions. But gradually the taut bonds of nervousness dissolved, and he talked freely about how he had burned away his youth and half his mature life in support of the communist ideal, and how it had been shattered by the Russian invasion.

"What you don't realize, you and other Western reporters," he said, "is that nearly 90 per cent of the Czechoslovaks were loyal Communists. Certainly we wanted to change the style and the meaning of communism, to make it less inhuman, to create a new society in Czechoslovakia which would allow ordinary people to realize their aspirations. But we never intended for a moment to swing the country back towards capitalism or even to take any steps that might be considered anti-Russian. When the Kremlin claimed it had to invade us to prevent the overthrow of the Communist party, it was a lie, because we never wanted to do that."

He went on to describe how, if the Dubcek initiative had been allowed to flourish, communism might have evolved into a genuinely popular political movement instead of a new form of dictatorship which concentrates power in the hands of party functionaries, how it could have pioneered an effective synthesis between the scientific revolution of our time and true socialism.

"And what happens now?" he asked. "For twenty-five years Czech thought and Czech journalism were concentrated on the notion that our country's future was bound up with our allies, the Russians. Will people ever again believe anything they read in the papers or hear from the politicians? Who will convince the next generation that there is any hope, any point to following the communist dogma?"

He reminisced about the spring of 1968, the exciting experience of being able to publish for the first time in his working life exactly what he thought, to read a free exchange of opinions. "The Russians have been claiming that the underground radio and television stations which stayed on the air after August 21, 1968, were part of a West German plot to take over Czechoslovakia," he said. "Some of the equipment was German, all right, but it consisted of ancient emergency transmitters left over from World War II, and stockpiled on Russian orders in the event of an invasion from the West. Of course, the irony that they should be used to fight an invasion from the East would be lost on the Russian mind; to appreciate irony, a people must be civilized."

After some more anti-Russian talk, he got up to go, suddenly impatient with me, himself, exhausted ideas, futile hopes, and vain heroics. "Most of us have left journalism now, because if we can't write the truth we don't want to write at all. Our slogan has become: 'Optimism equals lack of information.' But a few of the Dubcek followers are still trying to change things. After all, what can the Russians do except put them in prison? They can't invade us twice." [1970]

IV

A HARSH PRESENCE, with eyes as barren as potholes, Gustav Husak, who succeeded Alexander Dubcek as first secretary of the

Czechoslovak Communist party in April, 1969, does not comfortably fit the crucial role into which history has cast him. For Husak, described in the tortuous lexicon of Marxist ideology as "a moderate dogmatist", has become the only collateral the Czechs possesss against a return of their country to the darkness of neo-Stalinist oppression. He is certainly the best and probably the only chance the Czechs have of saving anything out of the Dubcek liberalization program and bringing their country back to something like economic health.

An austere, bespectacled bear of a man who raps out his sympathy for Czech nationalism and his disapproval for anything that departs from communist orthodoxy in the same sharp tones, Husak finds himself caught between two conflicting purposes. He must retain Russian support by persuading the Kremlin that he has permanently quashed the Dubcek progressives, while at the same time he must win acceptance among the Czechs by convincing them that he is not uncompromising in his anti-reform policies.

To gain the precious time he needs to achieve this delicate balance, Husak has been busy stroking the Czech populace with conciliatory words while acting tough enough to placate the Russians. In all his pronouncements, Husak is careful to differentiate between Dubcek's "romanticism" and his own "realism". He seems bent on leading his country by stealth into the modified liberalization achieved by Janos Kadar in Hungary. "Husak is just as concerned about people's duties as about their rights. But unlike the real hard-liners, he does remember that people still have rights," says one observer of Czech politics. "Certainly he's an orthodox Communist but so many liberals have been eliminated from the party's ruling circle here that of the survivors, Husak is well to the left of centre." Husak's most overt support of the Kremlin came last August when he put down riots marking the first anniversary of the Russian invasion by sending armed troops to dispel student protesters in Wenceslas Square. Immediately afterward, he was invited to Moscow, was awarded an Order of Lenin, and has been apparently carrying out Russian directives ever since.

The main reason he retains some degree of sympathy among the

Czechs is that he was himself a victim of the kind of oppressive measures the Russians are now trying to impose on his country. Born in 1913 near the Slovak capital of Bratislava, he joined the Communist party at twenty, fought the Nazis as a member of the Czech underground, and advanced in the postwar Communist hierarchy until 1950, when he was arrested on a charge of "bourgeois nationalism". Sentenced to life imprisonment, he was tortured, released only in 1960, and not allowed to return to active politics until 1967, when his Stalinist enemies in the Czech communist movement were on the run.

An early supporter of Dubcek, Husak became first secretary of the Slovak Communist party, and it was only after the dramatic events of August, 1968, that he turned against the reformers, calling the Russian invasion "an acceptable way out of the situation which will give us an opportunity to solve basic economic and national problems." Despite his orthodox communism, Husak's prison experience left him committed to supporting a framework of legality that will prevent the imprisonment of citizens without just cause. "We are not butchers and our party is not a slaughterhouse. It will never lower itself to contrived trials and contrived accusations — not even against political adversaries," he says.

But Czech intellectuals remain cynical. Though they doubt whether Husak will stage show trials based on confessions extracted by torture, he is quite capable, they think, of strangling party opponents in a web of petty legalisms. Husak's main problem at the moment is to surround himself with enough like-minded, relatively moderate followers so that he can go before next year's party congress (the 160-member ruling circle of the party) with a unified program that will have some chance of acceptance by both the Czechs and the Russians. His chief rival is Lubomir Strougal, who recently replaced the progressive Oldrich Cernik as the Czechoslovak premier. Strougal was one of the first Czechs to be sent to Moscow for secret-police training after the Communists took power in 1948, and he became minister of the interior in the Stalinist regime of Antonin Novotny. He later broke with Novotny and at one memorable central committee meeting, when Novotny chided him for his reputation as a ladies' man, Strougal shouted back, "It's true that these hands have held many a woman's behind. But they aren't bloody like yours."

Walking among Prague's old palaces, now occupied by the various communist ministries, you get a sense of intelligences at work behind their baroque facades but little feeling about the actual policies Czechoslovakia intends to follow in the future. Czechoslovakia's only hope now is for some form of long-term liberalization within the Kremlin itself which would be reflected in allowing part of Dubcek's program to be revived. But that seems at least a generation or so away. With the present too unbearable to think about, the Czechs live in the vague hope that tomorrow is bound to be better than today.   [1970]

V

THE CZECHS have never confused love of country with love of glory. They are the most ardently patriotic nationalists in central Europe, but they don't see much point in fighting wars they can't win. Throughout history (in 1848, 1938, 1948, and 1968) they have allowed their country to be invaded or taken over by outsiders but then confused their enemies with a subtle brand of insurrection that amounts to survival without heroics, collaboration without surrender.

The Czechs are very unsatisfactory subjects. There is at the moment in the Prague law courts, for example, a case being fought by a group of Czech lawyers who are demanding compensation from the Russians for the wooden traffic signs knocked over by their invading tanks two years ago. Because such audacity is not something the Russians know how to deal with, the Kremlin is rumoured to have agreed to pay a small indemnity. "When we win the case," one of the lawyers is being quoted around Prague, "we will, of course, give 220 roubles back to the Russians. That will take care of the return airplane fare for Dubcek from Moscow in 1968. After all, it was supposed to be a one-way ticket."

This mixture of quiet levity and relentless obstructionism, when practised on a national scale at every level of political and economic activity, can be devastatingly effective. "The victim suspects you are having him on, but he can't prove it," writes the American sociologist Milton Mayer in a recent study of the Czech character. "He has a monopoly on violence. But to be baited into using it, then crushing the joker, is to confess that he has nothing else. If the Czechs carry their serene imbecility too far and the Russians return to the cities shooting, they will convert their disaster into a cataclysm."

The Czechs do not subscribe to the Gandhian injunction of putting "one's whole soul against the will of the tyrant". Theirs is a much more subtle tactic. It is the art of what they call *pod fousky* which means "laughing under your moustache".

Heroism is something the Czechs have learned to outgrow. Their model is the Good Soldier Schweik, whose motto was: "Always try to outlive the enemy: dying will get you nowhere." Schweik was a fictitious batman in the Austro-Hungarian imperial army, the master creation of the Czech novelist Jaroslav Hasek. His misadventures make hilarious reading, but they reflect Schweik's supreme concern: to stay alive. He achieved such stunning success in keeping himself away from frontline fighting that, by the end of Hasek's book, he managed to be taken prisoner by his own army.

Schweikism is a kind of creative apathy which offers co-operation without actually delivering it. Obedience is loudly pledged but orders are invariably misunderstood. Schweik is always eager to comply with any and all demands made on him, but the net effect is the bafflement and confusion of his oppressors.

"Do you admit everything?" an angry Austrian officer asks the hapless Schweik.

"If you want me to admit it, sir, then I will. It can't do me any harm. But if you were to say: 'Schweik, don't admit anything, I'll argue to the point of my last breath.' "

At another interrogation, Schweik sums up his defence by solemnly and proudly declaring: "I'm no malingerer. I'm feeble-minded, fair and square. You just ask them in the Ninety-First Regiment."

Though the Russians make Schweik's Austrian superiors look pretty benign, the Czechs have successfuly adapted the Good Soldier's spirit to their present circumstances. In one current anecdote, a street cleaner comes up to a Russian soldier during a visit to Prague by Soviet Premier Kosygin, just as the Czech guard of honour is firing a twenty-four-gun salute. The street cleaner innocently asks, ''What's this — another war?''

''No, you imbecile. We have a V.I.P. visitor — Premier Kosygin.''

''In that case, what's wrong with our soldiers? They fired twenty-four rounds and missed him every time.''

Where Schweikism has become a serious threat to Czechoslovakia's Communist party is in the factories, on whose output the economy depends. Workers are staging deliberate slowdowns by misunderstanding orders and ostracizing those colleagues who want to fulfil production quotas. Absenteeism (always backed up by elaborate excuses) is running so high that the economy is now on a kind of unofficial three-and-a-half-day week.

The government of party secretary Gustav Husak has moved stringently against industrial malingering by sponsoring a new labour code that covers ''abuses of the socialist economy, working discipline and parasitism'', with a year's imprisonment for those found guilty. In true Schweikian fashion, workers are pledging their allegiance to Husak but not getting back to work. In union elections, they are placing silly loudmouths in important jobs while protecting their real leaders.

The Czechs have used these tactics to survive the colonialism of the Hapsburgs, the capitalist republicanism of Masaryk, the tyranny of the Nazis, and now the domestic socialist dictatorship of the Communists. Their will to survive has become their governing ideology, and it is as far as they want to commit themselves. Their spirit is a way of living out the Czech proverb that ''No man can tell in what faith he will die.'' [1970]

MAVIS GALLANT

When We Were Nearly Young

IN MADRID, nine years ago, we lived on the thought of money.
Our friendships were nourished with talk of money we expected to
have, and what we intended to do when it came. There were four of
us — two men and two girls. The men, Pablo and Carlos, were
cousins. Pilar was a relation of theirs. I was not Spanish and not a
relation, and a friend almost by mistake. The thing we had in
common was that we were all waiting for money.

Every day I went to the Central Post Office, and I made the
rounds of the banks and the travel agencies, where letters and
money could come. I was not certain how much it might be, or
where it was going to arrive, but I saw it riding down a long arc like
a rainbow. In those days I was always looking for signs. I saw
signs in cigarette smoke, in the way ash fell, and in the cards. I laid
the cards out three times a week, on Monday, Wednesday, and
Friday. Tuesday, Thursday, and Saturday were no good, because
the cards were mute or evasive; and on Sundays they lied. I thought
these signs — the ash, the smoke, and so on — would tell me what
direction my life was going to take and what might happen from
now on. I had unbounded belief in free will, which most of the
people I knew despised, but I was superstitious, too. I saw inside
my eyelids at night the nine of clubs, which is an excellent card,
and the ten of hearts, which is better, morally speaking, since it
implies gain through effort. I saw the aces of clubs and diamonds,
and the jack of diamonds, who is the postman. Although Pablo and

Pilar and Carlos were not waiting for anything in particular —
indeed, had nothing to wait for, except a fortune — they were
anxious about the postman, and relieved when he turned up. They
never supposed that the postman would not arrive, or that his
coming might have no significance.

Carlos and Pablo came from a town outside Madrid. They had
no near relatives in the city, and they shared a room in a flat on
Calle Hortaleza. I lived in a room along the hall; that was how we
came to know each other. Pilar, who was twenty-two, the youngest of the four of us, lived in a small flat of her own. She had been
married to Carlos's stepbrother at seventeen, and had been a
widow three years. She was eager to marry again, but feared she
was already too old. Carlos was twenty-nine, the oldest. Pablo and
I came in between.

Carlos worked in a bank. His salary was so small that he could
barely subsist on it, and he was everywhere in debt. Pablo studied
law at the University of Madrid. When he had nothing to do, he
went with me on my rounds. These rounds took up most of the day,
and had become important, for, after a time, the fact of waiting
became more valid than the thing I was waiting for. I knew that I
would feel let down when the waiting was over. I went to the post
office, to three or four banks, to Cook's, and American Express.
At each place, I stood and waited in a queue. I have never seen so
many queues, or so many patient people. I also gave time and
thought to selling my clothes. I sold them to the gypsies in the flea
market. Once I got a dollar-fifty for a coat and a skirt, but it was
stolen from my pocket when I stopped to buy a newspaper. I
thought I had jostled the thief, and when I said "Sorry" he nodded
his head and walked quickly away. He was a man of about thirty. I
can still see his turned-up collar and the back of his head. When I
put my hand in my pocket to pay for the paper, the money was
gone. When I was not standing in queues or getting rid of clothes, I
went to see Pilar. We sat out on her balcony when it was fine, and
next to her kitchen stove when it was cold. We were not ashamed
to go to the confectioner's across the street and bargain in fractions
of pennies for fifty grams of chocolate, which we scrupulously

shared. Pilar was idle, but restful. Pablo was idle, but heavy about
it. He was the most heavily idle person I have ever known. He was
also the only one of us who had any money. His father sent him
money for his room and his meals, and he had an extra allowance
from his godfather, who owned a hotel on one of the coasts. Pablo
was dark, curly-haired, and stocky, with the large head and opaque
eyes you saw on the streets of Madrid. He was one of the New
Spaniards — part of the first generation grown to maturity under
Franco. He was the generation they were so proud of in the
newspapers. But he must be — he *is* — well over thirty now, and
no longer New. He had already calculated, with paper and pencil,
what the future held, and decided it was worth only half a try.

We stood in endless queues together in banks, avoiding the bank
where Carlos worked, because we were afraid of giggling and
embarrassing him. We shelled peanuts and gossiped and held
hands in the blank, amiable waiting state that had become the
essence of life. When we had heard the ritual "No" everywhere,
we went home.

Home was a dark, long flat filled with the sound of clocks and
dripping faucets. It was a pension, of a sort, but secret. In order to
escape paying taxes, the owners had never declared it to the police,
and lived in perpetual dread. A girl had given me the address on a
train, warning me to say nothing about it to anyone. There was one
other foreign person — a crazy old Englishwoman. She never
spoke a word to me and, I think, hated me on sight. But she did not
like Spaniards any better; one could hear her saying so when she
talked to herself. At first we were given meals, but after a time,
because the proprietors were afraid about the licensing and the
police, that stopped, and so we bought food and took it to Pilar's,
or cooked in my room on an alcohol stove. We ate rationed bread
with lumps of flour under the crust, and horrible ersatz jam. We
were always vaguely hungry. Our craving for sweet things was
limitless; we bought cardboard pastries that seemed exquisite
because of the lingering sugary taste they left in the mouth.
Sometimes we went to a restaurant we called "the ten-peseta
place" because you could get a three-course meal with wine and

bread for ten pesetas — about twenty-three cents then. There was also the twelve-peseta place, where the smell was less nauseating, although the food was nearly as rank. The décor in both restaurants was distinctly un-European. The cheaper the restaurant, the more cheaply Oriental it became. I remember being served calves' brains in an open skull.

One of the customers in the ten-peseta restaurant was a true madman, with claw hands, sparse hair, and dying skin. He looked like a monkey, and behaved like one I had known, who would accept grapes and bananas with pleasure, and then, shrieking with hate at some shadowy insult, would dance and gibber and try to bite. This man would not eat from his plate. He was beyond even saying the plate was poisoned; that had been settled long ago. He shovelled his food onto the table, or onto pieces of bread, and scratched his head with his fork, turning and muttering with smiles and scowls. Everyone sat still when he had his seizures — not in horror, even less with compassion, but still, suspended. I remember a coarse-faced sergeant slowly lowering his knife and fork and parting his heavy lips as he stared; and I remember the blankness in the room — the waiting. What will happen next? What does it mean? The atmosphere was full of cold, secret marvelling. But nobody moved or spoke.

We often came away depressed, saying that it was cheaper and pleasanter to eat at home; but the stove was slow, and we were often too hungry to linger, watching water come to the boil. But food was cheap enough; once, by returning three empty Valdepenas wine bottles, I bought enough food for three. We ate a lot of onions and potatoes — things like that. Pilar lived on sweet things. I have seen her cook macaroni and sprinkle sugar on it and eat it up. She was a pretty girl, with a pointed face and blue-black hair. But she was an untidy, a dusty sort of girl, and you felt that in a few years something might go wrong; she might get swollen ankles or grow a mustache.

Her flat had two rooms, one of which was rented to a young couple. The other room she divided with a curtain. Behind the curtain was the bed she had brought as part of her dowry for the

marriage with Carlos's stepbrother. There was a picture of María
Felix, the Mexican actress, on the wall. I would like to tell a story
about Pilar, but nobody will believe it. It is how she thought, or
pretended to think, that the Museo Romantico was her home. This
was an extraordinary museum — a set of rooms furnished with all
the trappings of the romantic period. Someone had planned it with
love and care, but hardly any visitors came. If any did wander in
when we were around, we stared them out. The cousins played the
game with Pilar because they had no money and nothing better to
do. I see Pilar sitting in an armchair, being elegant and the boys
standing or lounging against a mantelpiece; I say "boys" because
I never thought of them as men. I am by the window, with my back
turned. I disapprove, and it shows. I feel like a prig. I tip the
painted blind, just to see the street and be reassured by a tram going
by. It *is* the twentieth century. And Pilar cries, in unaffected
anguish, "Oh, make her stop. She is spoiling everything."

I can hear myself saying grandly, "I don't want your silly fairy
tales. I'm trying to get rid of my own."

Carlos says, "I've known people like you before. You think you
can get rid of all the baggage — religion, politics, ideas, everything. Well, you won't."

The other two yawn, quite rightly. Carlos and I are bores.

Of them all, I understood Carlos best, but we quarrelled about
anything. We could have quarrelled about a piece of string. He was
pessimistic, and I detested this temperament; worse, I detested his
face. He resembled a certain kind of Swiss or South African or
New Zealander. He was suspicious and faintly Anglo-Saxon looking. It was not the English bun-face, or the Swiss canary, or the
lizard, or the hawk; it was the unfinished, the undecided, face that
accompanies the rotary sprinkler, the wet Martini, pussyfooting in
love and friendship, expense-account foolery, the fear of the open
heart. He made me think of a lawyer who had once told me, in all
sincerity, "Bad things don't happen to nice people." It was
certainly not Carlos's fault; I might have helped my prejudices,
which I had dragged to Spain with my passport, but he could not
help the way he looked. Pablo was stupid, but cheerful. Pilar was

demented, but sweet. What was needed—we agreed to this many times—was a person who was a composite of all our best qualities, which we were not too modest to name. Home from the Romantic Museum, they made me turn out the cards. I did the Petit Jeu, the Square, the Fan, and the Thirteen, and the Fifteen. There was happy news for everyone except Carlos, but, as it was Sunday, none of it counted.

Were they typical Spaniards? I don't know what a typical Spaniard is. They didn't dance or play the guitar. Truth and death and pyromania did not lurk in their dark eyes; at least I never saw it. They were grindingly hard up. The difference between them and any three broke people anywherelse was in a certain passiveness, as though everything had been dealt in advance. Barring catastrophe, death, and revolution, nothing could happen any more. When we walked together, their steps slowed in rhythm, as if they had all three been struck with the same reluctance to go on. But they did go on, laughing and chattering and saying what they would do when the money came.

We began keeping diaries at about the same time. I don't remember who started it. Carlos's was secret. Pilar asked how to spell words. Pablo told everything before he wrote it down. It was a strange occupation, considering the ages we were, but we hadn't enough to think about. Poverty is not a goad but a paralysis. I have never been back to Madrid. My memories are of squares and monuments, of things that are free or cheap. I see us huddled in coats, gloved and scarfed, fighting the icy wind, pushing along to the ten-peseta place. In another memory it is so hot that we can scarcely force ourselves to the park, where we will sit under elm trees and look at newspapers. Newspapers are the solace of the worried; one absorbs them without having to read. I sometimes went to the libraries—the British Institute, and the American one—but I could not for the life of me have put my nose in a book. The very sight of poetry made me sick, and I could not make sense of a novel, or even remember the characters' names.

Oddly enough, we were not afraid. What was the worst that

could happen? No one seemed to know. The only fear I remember
was an anxiety we had caught from Carlos. He had rounded
twenty-nine and saw down a corridor we had not yet reached. He
made us so afraid of being thirty that even poor Pilar was alarmed,
although she had eight years of grace. I was frightened of it, too. I
was not by any means in first youth, and I could not say that the
shape of my life was a mystery. But I felt I had done all I could with
free will, and that circumstances, the imponderables, should now
take a hand. I was giving them every opportunity. I was in a city
where I knew not a soul, save the few I had come to know by
chance. It was a city where the mentality, the sound of the language, the hopes and possibilities, even the appearance of the
people in the streets, were as strange as anything I might have
invented. My choice in coming here had been deliberate: I had a
plan. My own character seemed to me ill-defined; I believed that
this was unfortunate and unique. I thought that if I set myself
against a background into which I could not possibly merge some
outline would present itself. But it hadn't succeeded, because I
adapted too quickly. In no time at all, I had the speech and the
movements and very expression on my face of seedy Madrid.

I was with Pablo more than anyone, but I remember Carlos best.
I regret now how much we quarrelled. I think of the timorous, the
symbolic, stalemate of our chess games. I was not clever enough to
beat him, but he was not brave enough to win. The slowing down
of our respective positions on the board led to immobility of
thought. I sat nervously smoking, and Carlos sat with his head in
his hands. Thought suspended, fear emerged. Carlos's terror that
he would soon be thirty and that the affective part of his life had
ended with so little to show haunted him and stunned his mind. He
would never be anything but the person he was now. I remember
the dim light, the racket in the street, the silence inside the flat, the
ticking of the Roman-numbered clock in the hall. Time was like
water dropping — Madrid time. And I would catch his fear, and I
was afraid of the movement of time, at once too quick and too
slow. After that came a revolt and impatience. In his company I
felt something I had never felt before — actively northern. Seeing

him passive, head on hands, I wanted to urge and exhort and beg
him to do something: act, talk, sing, dance, finish the game of
chess — anything at all. At no period was I as conscious of the
movement and meaning of time; and I had chosen the very city
where time dropped, a drop from the roof of a cave, one drop at a
time.

We came to a financial crisis about the same moment. Pablo's
godfather stopped sending money to him—that was a blow. Pilar's
lodgers left. I had nothing more to sell. There was Carlos's little
salary, but there were also his debts, and he could not be expected
to help his friends. He looked more vaguely Anglo-Saxon, more
unfinished and decent than ever. I wished there was something to
kick over, something to fight. There was the Spanish situation, of
course, and I had certainly given a lot of thought to it before
coming to Spain, but now that I was here and down and out I
scarcely noticed it. I would think, "*I* am free," but what of it? I
was also hungry. I dreamed of food. Pilar dreamed of things
chasing her, and Pablo dreamed of me, and Carlos dreamed he was
on top of a mountain preaching to multitudes, but I dreamed of
baked ham and Madeira sauce. I suspected that my being here and
in this situation was all folly, and that I had been trying to improve
myself — my moral condition, that is. My financial condition
spoke for itself. It was like Orwell, in Paris, revelling in his
bedbugs. If that was so, then it was all very plain, and very
Protestant, but I could not say more for it than that.

One day I laid out forty-eight cards — the Grand Jeu. The cards
predicted treachery, ruin, illness, accidents, letters bringing bad
news, disaster, and pain.

I made my rounds. In one of the places, the money had come,
and I was saved. I went out to the University, where the fighting
had been, eleven or twelve years before. It looked like a raw
suburban housing development, with its mud, its white buildings
and puny trees. I waited in the café where Pablo took his bitter
coffee, and when he came in I told him the news. We rode into the
heart of Madrid on a swaying tram. Pablo was silent — I thought
because he was delighted and overwhelmed; actually, he must

have been digesting the astonishing fact that I had been expecting something and that my hanging around in banks was not a harmless mania, like Pilar in the Romantic Museum.

My conception of life (free will plus imponderables) seemed justified again. The imponderables were in my pocket, and free will began to roll. I decided, during the tram ride, to go to Mallorca, hire a villa, invite the three for a long holiday, and buy a dog I had seen. We got down from the tram and bought white, tender, delicious, unrationed bread, weighed out by the pound; and three roasted chickens, plus a pound of sweet butter and two three-litre bottles of white Valdepeñas. We bought some nougat and chestnut paste. I forget the rest.

Toward the end of our dinner, and before the end of the wine, Carlos made one bitter remark: "The difference between you and us is that in the end something will always come for you. Nothing will ever come from anywhere for any of us. You must have known it all along."

No one likes to be accused of posturing. I was as irritated as I could be, and quickly turned the remark to his discredit. He was displaying self-pity. Self-pity was the core of his character. It was in the cards; all I could ever turn out for him were plaintive combinations of twos and threes — an abject fear of anonymous threats, and worry that his friends would betray him. This attack silenced him, but it showed that my character was in no way improved by my misfortunes. I defended myself against the charge of pretending. My existence had been poised on waiting, and I had always said I was waiting for something tangible. But they had thought I was waiting in their sense of the word — waiting for summer and then for winter, for Monday and then for Tuesday, waiting, waiting for time to drop into the pool.

We did not talk about what we could do with money now. I was thinking about Mallorca. I knew that if I invited them they would never come. They were polite. They understood that my new fortune cast me out. There was no evasion, but they were nice about it. They had no plans, and simply closed their ranks. We talked of a longer future, remembering Carlos and his fear. We talked of our thirties as if we were sliding toward an icy subterranean water; as if we were to be submerged and frozen just as we were: first Carlos, then Pablo and me, finally little Pilar. She had eight years to wait, but eight would be seven, and seven six, and she knew it.

I don't know what became of them, or what they were like when their thirtieth year came. I left Madrid. I wrote, for a time, but they never answered. Eventually they were caught, for me, not by time but by the freezing of memory. And when I looked in the diary I had kept during that period, all I could find were descriptions of the weather.

GEORGE WOODCOCK

Encounter with an Archangel

I FIRST KNEW THE DOUKHOBORS as shadowy figures of legend in my English childhood, when my father would compensate for a dull life in a small town beside the Thames by weaving nostalgic threnodies on his young manhood in the Canadian west. Evenings on the prairies, with the great pink-bellied hawks settling down; Cobalt in the silver boom; fishing camps on the pristine shores of the northern lakes; and the great winter fires of the cities where burnt-out buildings became palaces of ice. Against such scenes the necessary characters moved in the cinema of my brain with the exaggerated gesticulation of Japanese actors. Lefty Louis and Zip the Blood shot it out with the police from a Winnipeg streetcar; Charlie Chaplin clowned through the one-elevator hamlets with Fred Karno; Chinese in blue gowns and pigtails scurried along Portage Avenue; strange Russians cleared snow in the prairie towns and were given to stripping in public, regardless of sex.

I realized the Doukhobors were something more than eccentric shovellers of snow when I read Tolstoy and Kropotkin and discovered that for these great Russians the Doukhobors were a group of admirable peasant radicals — Nature's anarchists. During the thirties I found in Doukhobor anti-militarism a strain that appealed to my own pacifism, and I accepted Tolstoy's impression of a libertarian sect who took their Christianity neat and had turned their settlements into Utopian communes. Like Tolstoy, I was unaware that this simple view took no account of certain fundamental aspects of Doukhobor philosophy and practice. Unlike Tolstoy, I learnt my error.

When my wife and I returned to Canada in the spring of 1949, I found that on Vancouver Island, where we settled, there was a small group of Doukhobors who had migrated from the interior of British Columbia and had founded a colony at Hilliers, sixty miles north of the village where we were clearing land and carpentering a house in search of that Tolstoyan *ignis fatuus,* the marriage of manual and mental work.

The people of our village talked reluctantly about the Hilliers community, yet even their hostile comments told us something. The leader of the group—a heretical offshoot—was a prophet who called himself Michael the Archangel. He openly preached the destruction of marriage, and this our neighbours vaguely envisaged as a complex and orgiastic pattern of shacking-up which provoked and offended their Presbyterian imaginations at one and the same time.

Since Hilliers was near, we could easily go there to see for ourselves, but we knew already that chronic bad relations with the Canadian authorities had made the Doukhobors distrustful of strangers. However, I wrote to the community, and by return I received a letter from the secretary, whose name was — almost predictably — Joe. He not only welcomed my interest, but invited us to stay at Hilliers as long as we wished. I was a little surprised at the enthusiastic tone of his letter, but the reason became evident once we reached Hilliers.

One day in August we set off northward, hitch-hiking, and it was late afternoon when the last driver turned off the seacoast road into the broad valley, hot and still of air, where Hilliers lies in the lee of the hard mountain spine that runs down the length of Vancouver Island. The older, non-Doukhobor Hilliers was a whistle-stop on the island railway, and the entrance to the community stood opposite a siding filled with boxcars. A high cedar fence faced the road. A large board was nailed to it. *Union of spiritual communities of Christ,* it said, in Russian and English. The wide gates stood open; looking between them, the eye encompassed and then recognized with some surprise the unconscious faithfulness with which a Russian village of the Chekhov era had been reproduced. Low cabins of logs and unpainted shacks were scattered along a faintly marked trail that ran between grass verges to end, a furlong on, at two larger two-storeyed houses standing against the brown background of the mountains, with the grey bubble of a communal baking oven between them. Each cabin was surrounded by a picketed garden, where green rows of vegetables and raspberry canes ran over the black earth in neatly weeded symmetry, and ranks of sunflowers lolled their brown and yellow masks towards the light.

An old woman with a white kerchief shading her face was hoeing very slowly in the nearest garden. She was the only person in sight, and I went up to her fence. Could she tell me where to find Joe? Her English was so broken that I could not follow what she was trying to tell me. By this time our arrival had been observed in the cabins, and a little wave of younger women in bright full petticoats, and of blond, crop-headed small boys, came towards us hesitantly. There was nothing of the welcome we had expected. Inge spoke to one of the women. "Joe ain't here," she answered. "He's at the other place." She waved vaguely northward. A pick-up truck drove in through the gates, and two young men got out. The women called to them, and they talked together in rapid, anxious Russian. Then one man got back into the truck and drove off, while the other came up to us. He was dark and nervous, dressed in an old blue serge suit, with chaff whitening the wrinkles. "I'm Pete," he said, "Joe's brother. Joe's coming." He paused. "Afterwards . . . you'll see Michael . . . Michael Archangel," he added hesitantly, and then fell silent. The small boys gave up interest and went to play in the boxcars.

Joe was so different from Pete that it was hard to believe them brothers — blue-eyed, wiry, jumping out of the truck to run and pump our hands. "Michael Archangel knew you were coming. A long time ago," he shouted. I had written only a week before. "A long time ago?" I asked. Joe looked at me and then laughed. "Yes, before you wrote!" Then he grabbed our rucksacks, helped us into the truck, and drove wildly for a couple of miles along a rough track beside the railway to a large old farm house in a quadrangle of shacks and barns surrounded by propped-up apple trees that were ochre-yellow with lichen. "This is the other place," Joe explained. "Most of the young people stay here. The old 'uns live up there with Michael Archangel."

We went into the kitchen. Two young women, fair and steatopygous as Doukhobor beauties are expected to be, were preparing the evening meal. A small girl showed us to our room and stood, avid with curiosity, while we unpacked our rucksacks and washed our faces. Then Joe took us around the yard, showed us the new bakehouse on which a hawk-faced man like a Circassian bandit was laying bricks, and tried to entice us into the bathhouse. I looked through the doorway and saw naked people moving like the damned in the clouds of steam that puffed up whenever a bucket of water was thrown on the hot stones. In a couple of seconds I withdrew, gasping for breath. The bricklayer laughed. "You never make a Doukhobor," he said. "Add ten years to your life," said Joe, coaxingly.

When everyone stood in a circle around the great oval table for the communal meal we began to see the kind of people the Doukhobors were. There were twenty of them, singing in the half-Caucasian rhythm that penetrates Doukhobor music, the women high and nasal, the men resonant as bells. Most had Slavonic features, their breadth emphasized among the women by the straight fringes in which their hair was cut across the brow. But a few, like the bricklayer, were so un-Russian as to suggest that the Doukhobors had interbred with Caucasian Moslems during their long exile in the mountains before they came to Canada. They sang of Siberian and Canadian prisons, of martyrs and heroes in the faith. "Rest at last, ye eagles of courage, rest at last in the arms of God," they boomed and shrilled.

The singing was solemn, but afterwards the mood changed at once and the meal went on with laughter and loud Russian talk; now and then our neighbours would break off repentently to translate for our benefit. The food was vegetarian, the best of its kind I have ever tasted; bowls of purple borscht, dashed with white streaks of cream, and then casha, made with millet and butter, and vegetables cooked in oil, and pirogi stuffed with cheese and beans and blackberries, and eaten with great scoops of sour cream. Slices of black bread passed around the table, cut from a massive square loaf that stood in the middle beside the salt of hospitality, and the meal ended with huckleberries and cherries.

Afterwards Joe and Pete took us to drink tea in a room they used as an office. It was furnished with a table and benches of thick hand-adzed cedar, but a big blue enamel teapot served instead of a samovar. This was the first of a series of long conversations in which the ideas of the community were imparted to us, principally by Joe, who spoke English more fluently than anyone else at Hilliers. Except for a few phrases, the details of the dialogues have become blurred in my memory during the thirteen years that have passed since then, but this, in substance, is what we were told on the first evening.

The community began with the experiences of Michael Verigin, a backsliding Doukhobor. Michael had left his home in the mountains, opened a boarding-house for Russians in Vancouver, and prospered there. After a few years Michael began to feel the malaise which many Doukhobors experience when they go from their villages into the acquisitive outside world, and he returned to the mountain valley of Krestova. Krestova is the Mecca of the Sons of Freedom, the fire-raising and nude-parading radical wing of the Doukhobor sect. Michael rejoined the Sons of Freedom and was regarded with deference because he bore the holy name of Verigin and was a distant cousin of Peter Lordly, the Living Christ who presided over the Doukhobors' first years in Canada, and died mysteriously in a train explosion during the twenties.

"Then Michael had a vision."

"A dream?"

"No, a vision. He was awake, and he said there was a voice and a presence."

"He saw nothing?"

"That time he didn't. The vision told him he was no longer

Mike Verigin. Michael the Archangel had gone into him. He was the same man, but the Archangel as well.''

"How did he know it was a real vision?"

"He just knew." Joe looked at me with the imperturbable blue-eyed confidence of a man used to assessing the authenticity of supernatural messages. "The vision said Michael must prepare the world for the Second Coming."

The Second Coming did not mean the return of Christ. According to Doukhobor belief, Christ is returning all the time in various forms. The Second Coming meant the establishment of God's earthly kingdom and the end of time and morality.

As the chosen pioneers in this great mission, the Doukhobors must purify themselves. The Archangel began by proclaiming that they must renounce not only meat and vegetables, but also tobacco and musical instruments. Joe himself had abandoned playing the violin, which he dearly loved. As he told me this, a radio was playing loudly in the kitchen. "That's O.K.," Joe reassured me. "A radio ain't a musical instrument."

Above all, the lust for possession must be rooted out. This meant not only a return to the traditional communistic economy from which the Doukhobors had lapsed under evil Canadian influences, but also the destruction of that inner citadel of possession, marriage. No person must have rights over another, either parental or marital. Women must be liberated, sexual relations must be free, families must wither away.

Two or three hundred of the Sons of Freedom, mostly seasoned old veterans of the nude marches and the pre-war internment on Piers Island, accepted the Archangel's teaching. Their neighbours showed disagreement by burning down the houses of those who followed Verigin. At this point the Archangel very conveniently had another vision.

Two of his followers must visit Vancouver Island. There they would find a town where a clock had stopped at half past two, and then they must proceed eastward until they saw a white horse by the gate of a farm. Joe and another man went on the expedition. They found the clock in Port Alberni, and the horse by the gate of a three-hundred-acre farm that was up for sale at a knockdown price. And, for what the fact is worth, I should record that after I had heard Joe's story I happened to visit Port Alberni, and there, on the tower of a fire-hall, I saw a dummy clock whose painted hands stood unmoving at half past two.

The farm was bought with the pooled resources of the faithful and Michael the Archangel led two hundred of his disciples on the exodus to Vancouver Island. Immediately after leaving the mainland he added to all the other prohibitions a ban on sexual intercourse—to conserve energies for the great task of spiritual regeneration. Complete freedom was only to be won by complete self-control. So much for the stories of Free Love rampant!

I wanted to find out the actual nature of the power that enabled Michael the Archangel to impose such restrictions. Tolstoy once thought that, because they opposed the state, the Doukhobors lived without rulers. Other writers had suggested that the Living Christs, like Peter the Lordly Verigin and his son Peter the Purger, had been rulers as powerful as any earthly governor.

"Michael is just our spiritual leader," Joe explained blandly.

"But he still seems to have a great say in your practical affairs."

"It depends on what you mean by *say*. He gives no orders. We are free men. We don't obey anybody. But he gives us advice."

"Do you always accept?"

"If we know what's good for us, we do."

"Why?"

"Because we know Michael the Archangel is always right."

"How do you know?"

"We just know."

The next day we met the Archangel. He had sent a message early that morning summoning us to his presence, and Joe drove us to the hamlet where we had arrived originally. The Archangel's house was one of the larger buildings, but we were not allowed to go in. We waited outside. The Archangel would meet us in the garden.

A tall man in his late fifties came stepping heavily between the zinnia borders. A heavy paunch filled his knitted sweater, and his shining bald head loosened into a coarse, flushed face with a potato nose, a sandy moustache, and small eyes that glinted out of puffy sockets. It was a disappointing encounter. The Archangel bowed in the customary Doukhobor manner, but without the warmth most Doukhobors put into their greeting. He shook hands limply. He spoke a few sentences in Russian, welcoming us and wishing us good health, and he affected not to understand English, though we learned later that he was effectively bilingual. He picked two small pink roses from a briar that ran along the fence and gave one to each of us. In five minutes he was gone, retiring with dignified adroitness and leaving our intended questions about archangelic power unanswered. Joe led us away, loudly declaring that the Archangel had been delighted with us, and that he had given many messages which he, Joe, would transmit in due course. Our whole relationship with the Archangel took on this elusive, indirect form, with Joe acting like a voluble priest interpreting and embellishing the laconic banalities of the oracle.

For the rest of the second day we wandered around the community, talking to the people we encountered. I pumped the handle of a primitive hand washing-machine, and learned from the girl I helped a curious instance of Doukhobor double-think. A spaniel bitch trotted over the yard, followed by a single pup. "She had four," the girl volunteered. "Did you give the rest away?" "No, they were drowned." "I thought you didn't believe in killing." "We didn't kill 'em. The Mountie sergeant drowned 'em for us." She chuckled, and quite obviously felt no guilt for merely condoning a killing someone else had carried out.

Under the prophetic discipline there were certain signs of strain. I found empty beer bottles in a corner of one Doukhobor field, and in the shelter of the ten-foot plumes of corn which were the community's pride a young man begged a cigarette and smoked in hasty gulps to finish it before anyone came in sight. Yet there was also an atmosphere of dogged devotion. Much of the land had been irrigated, and it was growing heavier crops of corn and tomatoes and vegetables than any of the neighbouring farms, while the houses were surrounded by rows of hotbeds and cold frames where

melons and gherkins ripened. The younger people talked constantly of schemes for new kinds of cultivation and for starting
light industries, but the younger people were so few. There were
too many children, too many old visionaries.

Sunday was the climax of our visit. Our arrival had coincided
with the community's first great festival. In the afternoon the only
child so far born there was to be handed over to the care of the
community as a symbolic demonstration against conventional
ideas of motherhood and the family. Since the Archangel had
forbidden fornication we were rather surprised that a being whose
very presence seemed to defy his will should be so honoured. From
my attempts to discuss the situation I gained an impression that the
Doukhobors applied a rather Dostoevskian equation—considering
that, if the ban itself was sacred, so must be the sin against it.
"Free men ain't bound by reason," as one young man rather
unanswerably concluded a discussion on this point.

The day began with morning service in the bare meeting house.
Flowers and plates of red apples had been brought in, and the
sunlight played over the white head-shawls and bright cotton
dresses of the women. Bread and salt stood symbolically on the
small central table, and also a great ewer of water from which
anybody who happened to feel thirsty would stop and drink as the
service went on. The women ranged to the right of the table and the
men to the left. On entering the hall each person bowed low from
the waist, and the bow was returned by the whole assembly; the
salutation was not to the man, but to the God within him. The
Archangel stood at the head of the men, benign and copiously
sweating; despite his celestial nature, he did not attempt to offend
Doukhobor precedent by acting like a priest. Today, in fact, as a
child was to be the centre of the festival, the children led off the
service, choosing and starting in their sharp, clear voices the
Doukhobor psalms and hymns for the day. Almost every part of
the service was sung, and the wild and wholly incomprehensible
chanting of the two hundred people in the small meeting house
produced in us an extraordinary sense of exaltation such as I have
only experienced once since then, in a church full of Zapotec

peasants at a festival south of Oaxaca. At the end of the service, we all linked arms at the elbows and kissed each other's cheeks, first right then left, in traditional token of forgiveness.

Later in the day we reassembled in the open air, forming a great V with the bread and salt at the apex. The singing rose like a fountain of sound among the drooping cedar trees, and between lines of women waving flowers and men waving green boughs the mother carried her child to the table. She was one of the young women we had met at the farmhouse on our arrival. As she stood there, her fair face grave and melancholy within the white frame of her head-shawl, she looked like the dolorous Mother of some naive ikon. The singing ended, the old hawk-faced bricklayer prayed before the table, and the mother, showing no emotion, handed the child to another of the women. The Archangel began to speak, in high, emotional tones; Pete, standing beside me, translated. The child would be named Angel Gabriel. The fruit of sin, he contained the seed of celestial nature. It was he who would fulfil the great destiny of the Doukhobors and lead mankind back on the great journey to lost Eden.

The women brought out pitchers of kvass and walked among the people as the orators began to speak. Emblematic banners were unfurled before the assembly. One, representing women dragging the ploughs that broke the prairies during the hard early days of the sect in Canada, was meant to celebrate the coming liberation of the sect from all forms of bondage. Another, covered with images of clocks and other symbols of time, was carefully expounded by the Archangel, who found in it the fatal dates that charted the destiny of the world. Then everyone spoke who wished — elders and young women; a Communist lawyer who had come in from the blue; even I, under moral coercion, as the enquiring Tolstoyan I then was. It was hot and tedious work as the sun beat down into the bowl among the mountains, and Sunday trippers from Qualicum Beach gazed in astonishment through the palisades.

We walked back to the farmhouse with a Canadian woman who had married into the Doukhobors. ''You've seen what Mike wants you to see,'' she said bitterly. ''You don't know all there is to know about that girl. Now she'll go up to stay in Mike's house. They won't let her talk to anyone, and they'll pay her out in every way they can for having a child by her own husband. Purification! That's what they talk about. I call it prison!'' The mother of the Angel Gabriel was not at the evening meal, and we never saw her again. We asked Joe what had happened to her. She had gone willingly into seclusion, he answered; for her own good, of course.

Indeed, Joe had more important things to talk about in that last conversation. "You have a great part to play in the future of mankind." He fixed me with a sharp, pale eye. "Michael's vision has told him that the end of the world is very near. Now we have to gather in Jerusalem the hundred and forty-four thousand true servants of God mentioned in Revelation. This time Jerusalem will be right here."

"Here? On Vancouver Island?"

"On this very spot."

"But how do you *know*?"

"We ain't worrying. We just know. And the Archangel had a vision about you. He knew you were coming a long time ago. He knew you were a writer. He knew you were being sent here so you could tell the world what we're doing."

I must have looked at him very dubiously, for he flapped his hands reassuringly. "I ain't asking you to do it. Nor is Archangel. We just know you will. You'll write about us, and people will come to us, and then you will come back and be marked with the sign and live for ever among the servants of God."

We left the next day. The Archangel saw us once more in the garden, gave us a white rose each, and said we should meet again before long. "It's a prophecy," Joe whispered.

And indeed it was. One day, months later, I was broadcasting in Vancouver when Ross McLean, who was then a radio producer, said he had heard Joe was locked up in the court house. I went over, but I could not see him. The Mounties were holding him incommunicado. But as I was leaving the station Michael the Archangel was brought in, and for a couple of minutes, in that grim barred room, I was allowed to talk to him. He was pleased to be recognized, and even willing to talk a little English. "I am free soon," he said, as he was led away to the cells. Not long afterwards he and Joe were sentenced on some rather nebulous charges of disturbing public order. And a few months later Michael the Archangel died in jail.

Ten years afterwards we drove through Hilliers, turning off our road on a nostalgic impulse. The palisade was still there, opposite the railway siding, and for a moment everything looked unchanged. But inside, where Jerusalem should have been rising, there was only the ghost of what we had seen on the day the Angel Gabriel was named. Most of the buildings had gone, but falling fences and squares of thistles still marked out the theocracy where the Archangel had ruled.

HUGH MAC LENNAN
By Their Foods . . .

DURING MY LIFE I have twice been asked by letter to tell what I like best to eat and why, my answers to be included in two separate publications. The requests were flattering, so I tried to narrow down my choices to some *pièce de résistance* by which, gastronomically speaking, I might become celebrated. In the end I welshed on my answers, for you might as well publish the results of your Rohrschach test as give a description of your favourite food. Favourite dishes can be as revealing as recurrent dreams; even the neophyte traveller learns as much about a nation's character by observing what its people eat as by talking for hours to its cab drivers.

Germans, for instance, have an obsession with caraway, and caraway lurks in every dish, a fatal undertone beneath the heavy, seemingly honest surface of German food, and you get into the habit of waiting for those black, curled little seeds to catch in your teeth, for the abrupt incongruousness of the caraway taste to shock your taste buds, just as you get into the habit of expecting a fatally recurrent behaviour-pattern to show up in German politics.

Austrians love pastries and whipped cream, succulent torten and rich brioches, bread with little nutriment but baked with crunchy crusts delicious to tongue and teeth. Charming they indubitably are, these people who suffer the tragedy of living just below a nation of caraway-eaters, and wise (or infatuated) in their determination to disguise the bitterness of life wherever possible. The coffee drunk by the Austrians is a dark and heavy brew, but as your taste dwells with the whipped cream floating on top, its bitterness is revealed only in the final drops.

Perfect in its ardour is the food of Italy. Not only the pizzas, spaghettis, macaronis, and raviolis with their divine harmonies of parmesan, ground meats, onions, tomatoes, and herbs, but the chianti, so honestly rough on the tongue it forms a bridge from the pastas to the fresh figs, oranges, tangerines, and walnuts that cap a true Italian meal — such a diet breeds people of a fine but delicate vanity, opera singers, and beautifully understanding women, but few successful lusters after power.

Most complicated, and complicated without being subtle is the diet of that intricate people, the Swedes. Strong, contrasting textures, robust flavours implicitly critical of each other, an immense variety of carefully thought-out detail enclosed within a single central idea — that is *smorgasbord*. The smoked eels, fish, and meats of Sweden are beyond compare, the pickles blunt but seldom sour, the vegetables fresh. Neither delicate nor rich, masculine but not uneasily so, neither one thing nor the other but everything simultaneously, all excellent, *smorgasbord* is the logical calculation of Swedish life.

Being a Swede, Swedes tell me, is not easy, because it means being a repository and practitioner of the best that has been taught, felt, discovered, and done in all the countries of the West, Sweden itself included. Being a successful Swede means that you have to be dynamic and static at the same time, tolerant and critical at the same time, jealous and magnanimous, virile and unaggressive all at once. The static intensity natural to Sweden can be observed in a Stockholm restaurant by anyone who watches a group of Swedes, grave and judicious, not so much attacking the *smorgasbord* as permitting their critical sense to play with this particular example of it. It is necessary for them to be sure whether the *smorgasbord* is as good as it ought to be or could be, and whether it is worthy of them and they of it, and when a foreigner sees a Swede in this condition the kindest thing he can do is to attack the *smorgasbord* himself. His enjoyment of it—or rather the fact that his enjoyment is so obvious—reassures the Swede both as regards the food of his country and his own feeling that he is more self-restrained than foreigners.

Of all the national diets I have sampled, the most portentous is the Russian. Those who eat heartily in Russia are few, or were few until very recently, but this makes no difference because these few are the only Russians who count. In 1937 I spent part of a summer in Leningrad and Moscow, eating in Intourist hotels, and even now when I remember the food and the people who enjoyed it, I tremble.

Russian food is almost exclusively protein, with a limited inter-larding of fat. At breakfast, which is served any time between nine and noon, I was offered five or six boiled eggs along with caviar, bread, and tea. At lunch, which dragged on from two in the afternoon until four-thirty, caviar was followed by *borsch* and topped by several courses of meat and fowl accompanied by tea. Dinner was more of the same except that it was much more, and the Russians who came to the hotel to eat generally settled down to their tables about midnight. After consuming huge slabs of pressed caviar, they worked their way through more *borscht*, more meat and fowl, and were offered (I can't remember whether it was before or after the meats) ponderous side dishes of head cheese, plates of smoked sturgeon, eels, and herring, and salmon pressed into shapes enriched with devilled eggs. While they chewed on-ward, they refreshed themselves with innumerable cups of pale tea, and most of them drank vodka and sweet Crimean champagne, and somewhere around two-thirty in the morning they at last stopped eating and went on their way. Only a people of colossal ambition and lack of subtlety could exist on such a diet, much less invent it. Churchill warned the world what to expect of Russia when he told us that Stalin, after eating a meal much larger than the one I have just described, settled down in his private quarters to an extra dinner consisting of a roast suckling pig. After eating the whole of it, he went back to work.

During all my time in Russia—this is the most significant note of all—I never saw a leaf of lettuce, or even a leaf of cabbage, that had not been turned into a heavy soup. One morning I woke up with the insides of my cheeks so swollen I couldn't close my jaws without biting chunks out of myself. From my boyhood reading of the life aboard sailing ships I knew this condition was caused by an excess of protein and an absence of fruit and greens. I searched for greens in vain, but I did manage to find some honey-dew melons kept by the *maître d' hôtel* as decorations on his sideboard. I bought three of them at two dollars apiece, and by midafternoon I was able to sit up and eat my caviar.

Chinese food, in the judgment of most travellers, is the finest there is, but to me it is decadent. Not in the way of the eating habits of the later Romans, of course; there is no record that the Chinese ever ate nightingales' tongues, or installed vomitoria as adjuncts to their banqueting halls, or that any Chinese emperor followed the example of Heliogabalus in promising a consulship or a province to the cook who invented a new sauce. Yet it is obvious that a man who enjoys thirty or forty courses for dinner, no matter how sparingly he may eat of each, is in danger of declining, even though his final fall may be accomplished with grace and a conviction that his previous life has been well spent. Chinese cooks on the grand scale seem to me not cooks at all, but Toscaninis of food, nor does anything give me more hope for the ultimate failure of Russian ambitions in China than the contrast between the tastes of these two peoples at table. Their incompatibility is total.

Of American cooking, apart from those restaurants in New York which offer specialities from all over the world, what can we say except that it is the most hygienic, scientifically balanced, and vitamin-conscious available? It is absolutely forthright, and no American dish above the Mason and Dixon Line ever pretends to be other than what it is. Nor is American food by any means as varied as Americans believe it to be, despite the thousands of recipes published yearly in women's magazines, for variety is bound to be limited when both cook and eater agree that what counts as the final standard of excellence is the quality of the raw materials, and when nearly everybody wants to top off with ice cream. Only in New Orleans, where a Creole tradition in decline united with a climate that often spoiled uncooked food, do you find any exaggerated development of highly flavoured sauces. Throughout the rest of the country steaks from the primest of beeves, chickens guaranteed tender by metal tags, salad-greens and vegetables scientifically grown and Cellophane-wrapped for the market, potatoes mealy and incomparable from Maine and Idaho — American food is as direct as American prose literature and (so say European connoisseurs) American love-making.

Of all the foods I know, the most fascinating is the English, for like everything else English, it cannot be considered apart from history, nor is its message in any sense as simple as it seems. While the empire was a-building, Englishmen ate massive meals of protein and starch, but once the empire was built, the English ruling classes tried to come to terms with a dilemma their knowledge of history told them was critical for their national existence. If they enjoyed the pleasures of the table too much (and now they could utilize all the diets known to man) they would lose their empire for the same reason the Romans lost theirs. Yet what was the use of the empire if it condemned them to living permanently on Brussels sprouts?

The ruling class of England thereupon came to a typically English compromise. Indifferent to the lower classes, themselves accustomed to spending at least a month of every year on the Continent where they could eat the delicious foods of decadence, they decided to outdo Sparta within the home island, nor was any law necessary to guarantee the moral salubrity of English restaurant food. By that extrasensory perception which enables the island to survive, English cooks saw their duty and did it. Hence the boiled meats and fish, the cabbages and sprouts dripping with lukewarm water, the incredible gooseberry fools, the one all-purpose sauce that looks like ground caterpillars and is used to lubricate everything erroneously called a sweet. But those foreigners who believe the English drink the kind of coffee they do because they lack the wit to make it any other way, have as much understanding of the English mentality as the German admiral who believed the Grand Fleet held the seas after Jutland only because the British were too stupid to know they had been beaten.

If a wise maturity accounts for the food of England, masochism must be held responsible for what the Scotch eat. Believe no Scotchman who tells you that his countrymen can afford no better. When Lord Strathcona was a millionaire many times over, oatmeal porridge, so I am told, remained his favourite dish. Believe no Scotchman who attributes the national diet to the barrenness of Scottish soil. Scotland is surrounded by billions of the finest food fish in the world, and the Scotch are skilled fishermen. If they boil their salmon and halibut till no taste remains, if they bake out of their haddock the last drop of moisture, if they serve these ruined fish with a dry, grey potato and (for variation) boiled turnips and sprouts, if they offer for dessert soggy rice pudding with bloated raisins bulging out of it, if they equate a distaste for haggis with disloyalty to Scotland herself — let nobody pity them or wonder why they eat as they do. They prefer this diet because it gives them the pleasure of being miserable.

As I neither need nor dare discuss the cooking of France, I come finally to what I would call, were I Jonathan Swift, my own dear country.

A few years ago an article appeared in one of our national magazines which asserted that Canadian cooking, apart from that of Montreal, is the most tasteless in the world and the most carelessly prepared. In a later article in the same magazine statistics were paraded to establish a corollary to the previous hypothesis — namely, that Canadians are the greatest eaters of ketchup known to the Heinz company and that there are many Canadians who eat ketchup three times daily.

The only thing that astonished me about these articles, especially the former one, was the public response they occasioned. The editor was buried under a deluge of letters written by furious housewives and loyal males boasting about their mother's apple pies. Here, indubitably, was evidence that Canada is in the throes of a moral revolution.

A generation ago most Canadians would have been quietly pleased with a writer who told the world that their food is tasteless and carelessly prepared. Puritanism in Canada was not on the defensive then, and the reading public would have taken "taste-

less" to mean "wholesome" and "carelessly prepared" to indicate that we are a people with no nonsense about us, reserving our
full energies for things higher than sensual pleasures, of which the
pleasures of the table are unquestionably the lowest. Now, it
seems, we are almost willing to admit that cooking is an art we may
begin to practise one of these days, and that perhaps it might be
interesting to climb a few steps up the slippery slope called civilization.

Psychologists have been heard to murmur that the desserts of
our childhood are the dishes we most yearn for in our adult lives,
and that this is why even middle-aged and elderly Scotchmen
continue to eat rice puddings no matter how rich they are. If we
don't get our childhood desserts, so they say, it is because our
wives do not care for them or they have gone out of fashion. But
with all respect for my own childhood, which was not an unhappy
one, I harbour no nostalgic longing for the cold baked-apple and
tapioca pudding which invariably made its appearance, one or the
other, whenever I visited relations or dined out with a boyhood
friend. In our own house these were eschewed, at least as a rule,
and personally I suffered little from the puritan theory that pleasure
in food is a sin. It was the society all around me I am talking about
here, not my own home, for the strength of character that made
Nova Scotia great was absolutely determined to impress upon
children the salutary knowledge that if they really enjoyed what
they eat it was probably bad for them, while if they loathed the
taste of it, they were being well nourished. So now, as I can no
longer postpone answering those letters asking for my favourite
menu, I shall do so in detail and with candour.

For breakfast I like a half-partridge, *petit pois* underdone, some
light greens and a half-bottle of hock. For lunch I will make do
with a small serving of lobster Newburg or a golden-brown *soufflé*
high as a chef's cap and enclosing within its airy mystery a nest of
soft-boiled eggs—I ate this once in my life and have never been the
same man since. Champagne is a daylight drink with me; I like it
best with such a lunch at a table where no politics are discussed.
Tea I dispense with unless I am in England, and as I have been in

England only for a few weeks in these last many years, let's say I dispense with afternoon tea entirely, for it is a poor preparation for the dry sack I like before dinner but almost never drink. Dinner is, of course, the solace of a hard day, and I prefer it accompanied by a variety of wines, mostly white, and a really good dinner I like to see articulated with some of the subtlety one looks for, but seldom finds, in a well-worked novel. The oysters should be Malpèques untouched by any sauce, and the meal should continue through vichyssoise on to Dover sole, airborne to Montreal and cooked so lightly I can still taste the North Sea (so subtly different in taste to the western Atlantic) in its incomparable flesh. For the climax to this dinner I should like roast pheasant or woodcock, and before the *demi-tasse* of Turkish coffee prepares my palate for a few dry *fines,* I choose something light, brief, and *flambant* for a sweet, followed by a small but knowledgeable morsel of *brie* or of a soft cheese of rare delicacy native to the Ile d'Orléans. Let psychologists make of this what they will.

WILDER PENFIELD

The Superiority of the Bilingual Brain

THE HUMAN BRAIN is not a previously programmed calculator. It is a living, growing, changing organ. It can even carry out its own repairs to some extent. But it is subject to an inexorable evolution of its functional aptitudes. No one can alter the time schedule of the human brain, not even a psychiatrist or an educator. The built-in biological clock tells the passage of opportunity for teacher and parent.

When I was in India in 1957, visiting some of the universities under the Commonwealth Colombo Plan, I received a startling invitation from the Department of Education to give a series of two broadcasts over the All-India Radio on the teaching of secondary languages. Some educator, I reflected, must indeed be desperate. It might well have been so, for the Government of India had laid at the door of the Ministry of Education the task of teaching the people Hindustani and English, although the mother tongue of the majority was something else. The request was startling to me, not because the problem was new but because an educator was evidently giving some thought to the physiology of the human brain.

My wife tried to reassure me by pointing out that our own children had gained a satisfactory command of two added languages. We had done no more than to have them hear German and French well spoken in their early childhood. Was it, after all, as simple as that? I gave the broadcast, and the Department of Education had copies of it printed and distributed to the teachers of India.

For my own part, I had heard no foreign tongue before the age of sixteen. After that, I found it necessary to study three modern languages for professional purposes, but I spoke none well. Before beginning the study of medicine, I even spent a whole year teaching German, and was paid for it, in an otherwise efficient boys' school. It was, I fear, very poor language teaching. I handed on, as best I could, the words and the grammar I had learned at Princeton, to boys who were between fifteen and eighteen years of age.

On the other hand, my own children learned to use German and French without apparent effort, without foreign accent, and without the long hours of toil that I had sacrificed to language study. They did well what I did badly. There must be a psychological explanation for the difference (unless these children were vastly more intelligent than their father!).

Before saying anything more about the children or the broadcast in India, perhaps the reader will follow me in a short detour. I have had a remarkable opportunity to study speech mechanisms, language learning, and bilingualism. Most of my clinical career has been passed in Montreal where my patients were half French-speaking and half English-speaking. I have seen children, below the age of ten or twelve, lose the power of speech when the speech convolutions in the left hemisphere of the brain had been destroyed by a head injury or a brain tumour. I have seen them recover after a year of dumbness and aphasia. In time, they spoke as well as ever because the young child's brain is functionally flexible for the start of a language. They began all over again. Occasionally we were able to study what had happened. In every case, we found they had established a speech centre located on the other side of the brain in what is called the non-dominant hemisphere. (In a right-handed person, the left hemisphere is normally dominant for speech. That is, it contains the whole specialized speech mechanism.)

When the major speech centre is severely injured in adult life, the adult cannot do what he might have done as a child. He may improve but he is apt to be using the remaining uninjured cortex on the side of the injury. He can never establish a completely new centre on the non-dominant side, as far as our experience goes. That is not because he is senile. It is because he has, by that time, taken over the initially uncommitted convolutions on the non-dominant side of his brain for other uses.

Man has, in his brain a remarkable increase in convolutions that are not committed to sensory or motor function, as compared with other animals. In the temporal regions, if they are not used in the creation of a speech mechanism, they are gradually devoted to perception. Before the child begins to speak and to perceive, the uncommitted cortex is a blank slate on which nothing has been written. In the ensuing years much is written, and the writing is normally never erased. After the age of ten or twelve, the general functional connections have been established and fixed for the speech cortex. After that, as I have pointed out, the "non-dominant" area that might have been used for speech is now fully occupied with the business of perception.

The brain of the twelve-year-old, you may say, is prepared for rapid expansion of the vocabulary of the mother tongue and of the other languages he may have learned in the formative period.

In my broadcast to the teachers of India, I could only reason as follows: Do not turn without question to the West for your model of teaching secondary languages. Consider first the changing functional capacities of the child's brain. Most of our schools in the West begin the teaching of foreign languages by the dead-language technique. It was designed for adults learning Greek and Latin by means of word lists and grammar. Your hope that the people of India will speak English and Hindustani as living languages is doomed to failure if you follow this technique. The dead-language techniques has its place, no doubt, but it cannot be used in the early years when the child is a genius at language initiation.

But there is another method of beginning a language—the direct method that mothers use. It was used to teach foreign languages as well as the mother tongue, in the families of ancient Ur and in those of the Roman Empire. It is used by some parents in the West and in the East today. Even a child's nurse or the least experienced tutor can use the mother's method for a second language. The mother does her teaching when the child's brain is ready for it. In three or four years she may only give the child a few hundred words, perhaps. But he gets the set, acquires the units, creates the functional connections of the speech cortex. In unilingual countries the mother conducts the first stage of language learning by the direct method and the school carries on easily with the second stage, vocabulary expansion. If a nation is to be bilingual or trilingual or multilingual, the nation's schools should adopt the mother's direct method for the first stage of foreign-language teaching.

In presuming to offer a solution to the teachers of India, I was speaking from scientific evidence.[1] But I also spoke as a man who had tried unsuccessfully to master secondary languages by the classical methods, or as a teacher of German who had employed the classical method, or, finally, as a father whose children had approached two second languages successfully by the mother's method. In any case, I ventured the following opinion:

India's problem is not insuperable. Use the mother's method at the very beginning of formal education with teachers who can speak either English or Hindustani well and who understand kindergarten techniques. Following that, I outlined, in a rather confused manner (my thinking was less clear in this regard then than now), what I have described as parallel bilingualism (one language in the morning, the other in the afternoon).

But India, with her most important task of language teaching, is far away. In other nations of the world the problem of second-language teaching is hardly less urgent, although it presents itself in varying patterns. There is a good deal of evidence to suggest that when a young child is allowed to hear a second language and learns to use only a few hundred words of that language, he becomes a better potential linguist; his uncommitted cortex is conditioned to further second-language learning. It is difficult or impossible to condition it thus later in life because the functional connections tend to become fixed.

This would explain the reputed genius of the Swiss, the Poles, and the Belgians as linguists. Most of them hear a second language in early childhood, in the streets and the playgrounds, if not at home. On the other hand, the average so-called Anglo-Saxon in

Great Britain or the United States hears only English until, possibly, he is taught a modern language in his teens at school.

J. B. Conant (former President of Harvard), in his studies of American high schools, concluded that in the best schools of today the work is satisfactory except in one department, the teaching of foreign languages. The classical method, with its grammar and word lists designed to teach dead languages, is the method of the high school. A little child cannot use it. He would only laugh at it, and yet the little child is the genius in our society for starting languages.

Educators, to be scientific, must consider the physiology of a child's brain. When the classical method is used to start a unilingual teenage pupil or adult in the learning of second languages, the procedure is not in accordance with the dictates of neurophysiology. With hard work, it may serve the purpose. But it is no more than a second-best method.

The mother's technique is used for adults, for example, in the Berlitz method, with reasonable success. Conversation courses for teenagers in school can be successful, when they are well done, even after the age of twelve. But these methods are far more successful if the student has heard a second language early in life.

The experience of many parents has, of course, been similar to our own, past and present. It is a common experience that when families immigrate, the children learn the new language by the direct method (without confusion) and unilingual parents learn it less well and more slowly by translation and with a mother-tongue accent. This is the supporting evidence of common experience.

And yet there are those who argue that it is better for a child to establish the mother tongue well before confusing him by exposure to a second language! Actually, the child seems to be protected from confusion by rapidly acquired conditioned reflexes and by the action of the "switch mechanism", which is a conditioned reflex.

There is good evidence that familiarity with additional languages, even though limited, in the first decade, endows the normal child with a more efficient and useful brain. In a study conducted under W. E. Lambert, Professor of Psychology at McGill University, it was concluded recently that bilingual children, at the ten-year level in Montreal, showed no confusion and some evidence of greater intelligence than unilingual children of the same age. They were examined by non-verbal as well as verbal tests.[2]

Another study has been carried out in the same department.[3] In this study, an equal number of bilingual university students was compared with a similar selection of unilingual students. The bilingual students scored higher in intelligence tests when those tests were verbal and also when they were non-verbal. In the bilingual society of the Province of Quebec, those who were bilingual before entering university would have heard the second language early.

While the mother is teaching the child to understand and to use a few hundred words and teaching the child to perceive the meaning of words and experiences, she is "programming" the brain. Part of the uncommitted cortex is being conditioned or programmed for speech, the remaining uncommitted cortex is used as a part of the mechanism of perception. In the second decade of life, functional connections seem to have become fixed. Vocabulary expansion and multiplication of perceptions then proceed rapidly.

The mother's method of direct language teaching can be used for second languages but this should *begin* before the age of six or eight if possible. When the uncommitted cortex is conditioned early, the individual becomes a better linguist; the child is better prepared for the long educational climb. In the years of life that follow, man or woman will more easily become the "well-educated" adult for which the future calls so urgently.

From South Africa, where bilingualism is much more general than it is in Canada, comes additional evidence. E. G. Malherbe, the recently retired Vice-Chancellor of Natal University, made a detailed study, some years ago, of eighteen thousand pupils in schools conducted in both English and Afrikaans. He concluded that the bilingual and the trilingual students did significantly better in the tests given to them than the unilingual ones. This applied to the verbal tests and to the non-verbal tests alike, and his work was critically controlled.[4]

Professor Malherbe visited Montreal in 1967. His conclusions, I discovered with delight, were identical to my own, although his evidence was quite different. Expressed in a few words, our conclusions were: An early second-language start improves intellectual performance in the later stages of education. The way to make a country bilingual is to let the children hear the second language very early.

This does not detract from the academic performance in the mother tongue but gives him a real advantage. It enriches family culture and gives it strength. It increases earning power.

The advantages of a bilingual brain are not alone the greater ease in learning and using other languages and the greater knowledge of other cultures than that of the child's parents. There is also significant evidence of better general performance in other departments of education. Here is a field in which university and high-school surveys must test the wisdom of those who plan elementary education and the curriculum of kindergarten and the first year of school.

It is the genius, the inherited aptitude, of the little child that, when he hears a language spoken, he programs his computer for future intellectual activity. To do this he is pre-empting and preparing certain uncommitted areas of the brain for intellectual activity of the highest type.

All children should hear a second language before the age of six or eight if they are destined for something more than elementary education. And indeed if they are not. If they are to join the less-educated class, bilingualism will still serve the purposes well, and it is so easy to acquire! And now, to conclude:

Teachers and parents must always share responsibility for the education of each new generation. This includes the initial programming of each child's brain. It prepares the man for great achievement or limits him to mediocrity. A neurophysiologist can only suggest that the human brain is capable of far more than is demanded of it today. Adjust the time and the manner of teaching to the aptitudes of the growing, changing master-organ. Then, double your demands and your reasonable expectations.

NAIM KATTAN

The Word and the Place
(translated by Alan Brown)

IN THEIR OSCILLATIONS between perpetual nostalgia and the loss of some portion of themselves, few voluntary exiles recover entirely from their banishment. I chose to leave one civilisation and adopt another: one more individual adventure, obscured or diminished to the vanishing-point in the total flood of immigrants.

No one can change the language he speaks, the bread he eats, the colour of his sky, without his very substance being thrown into confusion; without his newly vulnerable being revealing its secrets; without his mystery, ignored until now because taken for granted, being exposed in all its fragility. Very few are able to resist. One begins to search for any kind of new security, even if one must settle for no more than the surface of old certainties. The voluntary exile must forget who he is, and pretend to follow a rhythm out of phase with his own. Otherwise he isolates himself — though the isolation is mitigated by a new everyday life — within his own secret, living out in exile a diminished reality composed of nostalgia and rites or customs that seem more and more anachronistic. He has no choice but to forget himself, if he wants to live out his fate completely and not avoid it. He is a shared, a divided man, who finds in his distress a new balance that brings with it energy and richness greater than all those blindly given by a rooted existence.

In the anonymity of his own collectivity he does not think about his identity: is it anything more than his surname, his work, his family status? Transplanted, these things are not indications of belonging, they are symbols of difference. I am not speaking of those who are obliged by political or economic circumstances to leave their country and make a new start elsewhere; or rather I speak only of those among them who attempt to turn a forced exile into a choice, opting consciously not for a new anonymity, nor for a useless and illusory fidelity to their past, but for a division of their being.

Lived to the full this choice takes a modern man along a path quite different from those of anonymity or the putting down of roots. Is this path a new hope? Success is uncertain and the rewards fragile. We are talking about a process, a state of mind, an openness to life, not about a mechanism with predictable consequences.

If I exile myself voluntarily I consciously put myself in a vulnerable state. The resulting torment is my way of rejecting emptiness, of recreating my being in risk and danger. If I put my most private self on the line it is perhaps so that I may remain aware of it, so that it does not imperceptibly disappear. First to be risked is the mirror of my privacy: my means of expression.

Changing one's language means more than mastering a new one. I can be perfectly polyglot in my own country; on trips or visits abroad I can converse in languages far removed from my own. Then other languages are a kind of knowledge that opens doors for me, vehicles that make exchanges possible. That has nothing to do with my decision to make a foreign language my primary tool of expression. The effects are profound, even though they are imperceptible at the beginning.

I learned French in Baghdad. But I wrote in Arabic, and saw myself already as one of the artisans of a literary revival in my country. French, a foreign tongue, opened new and liberating horizons. World culture seemed to be within my reach. In Paris this language became an instrument for daily use, an immediate and natural fact. Without my realising it, the field of my mother-tongue shrank. Arabic was kept for conversations with my countrymen. Speaking French all day long, I was furious when I had to speak it with a classmate from Baghdad because we happened to be with a Frenchman. In our native city this would have been a simple matter of courtesy. In Paris it was a revelation of the change in value that our language had undergone. It was now a distant, exotic phenomenon. Only when I was writing — in Arabic — did I rediscover my private world and feel completely myself again. I wrote about my new city, I wrote about the French. Now I could reverse the situation: it was the French who were exotic creatures requiring explanation. I rediscovered the complicity of words. A public that I could imagine was there before my eyes. I was no longer in Paris, or at least only temporarily, on some kind of errand. As I wrote I reoccupied my own universe, I won back my country word by word.

The attraction of France was too great: I could not succumb to the enticements of exile. I now tried to reverse the earlier process: I wanted to communicate in French what was nearest to my heart, to translate to the West my reality as an Oriental. But we cannot switch languages without a revolution in our inner life. To possess the French language and live within it, to manipulate it from the inside meant a total change in my rapport with reality. Certain images were ineradicable. And gross mistakes that persisted despite a long apprenticeship denoted the survival of a vision of the world that I had consciously and voluntarily traded for another. Even if I no longer say *le lune* or *la soleil*, the sun for me remains inalterably the sun of my childhood: it belongs to the feminine kingdom, and the moon to the masculine. Arabic and French are poles apart in the relationships they establish with reality. Arabic, a language in which conceptualisation is a borrowed function, makes no use of the adjective because it is foreign to its genius. Arabic is the language of the thing named, not the thing qualified. The image replaces the adjective, and when an adjective is used it never has the precision it possesses in languages derived from Greek or Latin.

I came to French encumbered by the heavy baggage of Arabic. French was a fragile instrument which I could at any moment either transform by the magic of another language, or bury under a florid style. From this time on I explored the tortuous ways of my

own language like a French tourist, with a learned but imprecise
air, for my new precision was borrowed. Writing in two languages
had become an impossibility. I lived simultaneously in two
worlds, with a resultant tension that at times was intolerable,
occasionally beneficial. To write in two languages without one
becoming an echo or reflection of the other would have required a
useless effort I was not prepared to make. I no longer lived in the
Orient, because I refused to consider myself an exile in France.
The old world I bore within me, but I felt free in the new, because
as soon as I succeeded in making it my own it became a second
reality for me. I saw no further need to write in Arabic. I could no
longer struggle against my need to live in the French universe. But
on what conditions could I live there? At this moment my real
emigration began. Pressures were there, and increasing: should I
change my name, never again speak Arabic, declare myself haugh-
tily and proudly occidental, consign the Orient to oblivion or
contempt? It was out of respect for the world I was entering that I
wanted to preserve what was most precious from my former world,
the direct access to intimacy. One can only change languages in
full awareness of what is involved, measuring what is left behind,
what has been abandoned. Otherwise there is no change of language, merely a change of the vehicle of conversation. One does
not immigrate from one culture to the other, though one can move
from one city to another.

Avoiding the tensions would have led to a loss of self. Only in
tension can one hew out a place in the new language, this unknown
land that the explorer alters as he discovers it, making of it not a
stopover or an invisible decor, but an inhabited place. Languages
cannot be superimposed nor do they cohabit separately. They grow
together: one invades the other, informs the other, pressing it from
within to the bursting point. The separate man who chooses and
accepts his separateness ends by living beneath a double mask, and
a mask does more than protect integrity and privacy against intrud-
ers; it also raises a screen between man and reality. The division of
his being, once accomplished, forces him into theatre. He wel-
comes a new world effusively in order to make tolerable an

existence which he does not really choose, and at the same time he idealises a previous world in which he no longer believes, even if he convinces himself that he will one day return to it. The dilemma of the divided man is that he becomes accustomed to living in a double dramatisation, and even when he returns to his native country it no longer seems real to him; it becomes bearable only if it is transformed in turn to a stopover in relation to his second world, and embellished by nostalgia as is every theatrical universe.

In Montreal *le genièvre hollandais* becomes *du gros gin,* and if oranges from Baghdad were imported to this city they would lose their savour. The traveller delights in the surprises of foreign tastes, but this is inverted homesickness, for he reassures himself by dreaming of the certainties of his national cuisine. If in his home city he seeks out from time to time the exotic dishes of other countries, it is by his own choice, and he has no need to abandon or modify his relationship with the products of nature.

When I was in Baghdad the insistence of western poets on the beauties of springtime seemed to me a little exaggerated. Even lyricism and imagination, I thought, should have a limit. Our fruit was not imported, and when friends coming back from vacations in the north brought us the over-sized peaches that grew there, we knew that what we were tasting was foreign and did not belong to our world. And when I passed a store frequented by the foreign colony (mainly British), overflowing with European fruit, tinned food, spices, and delicatessen products, I knew there was no point in my crossing the threshold. These things were not intended for me. One day, tired of knowing the West through books alone, and wanting to experience the smell of it, I entered as though going on a voyage. I never went back. I hadn't been after a change of scene, or some exotic thrill, and I found in this fraction of Europe only doors that opened on unreality.

Later I knew the sea, the rains of summer, springtime, snow. . . . I was always tempted to take refuge in the relativity of seasons and climates, with the desert and its scorching heat as my yardstick in the diversity of nature, so that another sky might seem more pure, another climate less hostile. But one has not yet left a country if it remains the measure for all others. To emigrate is to tear oneself deliberately away from immediate reality and the external world, without turning nature into a stage-set. To emigrate is to plunge consciously into a new winter, a different summer, to forget the taste of fruit only to discover it again, to die in order to live again, to bury one life in memory so that another can flower. Then nature loses its innocence. From that moment our reaction to it ceases to be instinctive. It is a learned reality, discovered, autonomous. Now we know that spring exists because we have experienced its absence. And we do not take the plunge in innocence, for we do not live in immediate intimacy with nature and its relativity, but in a series of deaths and rebirths. I know now that it is possible to live without having experienced the desert, or without mountains, or without snow. But the earth is not a fatherland that we carry in our hearts, nor is it a changing backdrop. On it we live out our death and our birth, our fragility and our permanence, approaching but never reaching the promised land of a marriage of man and nature. If the external world is not to become theatre, each tree, each fruit, each season is final and unique, and I must tear myself away from the familiar, transform myself by changing worlds, lose myself, find myself again, accumulating successive realities without confusing them.

When we are no longer tempted to set ourselves over against nature in order to protect our autonomy, home becomes possible; a city is no longer a stopover. Jerusalem is the city of perpetual desire, Rome the dwelling place of a church and Mecca a rallying point and pilgrim's goal. There have been many attempts to transform a particular spot into a chosen place where man will surpass himself, a place that is not a symbol but an incarnation, a station for what is transcendent. One can go anywhere in the world bearing a new Jerusalem. One can carry forever the sign of a visit to Mecca, home of the last prophecy. Pilgrims there complete their religious duty by touching the sacred place with their foot. They are transformed, and their privileged relationship with nature is not an ephemeral moment but a stage in their total journey, one that transforms them by transforming their link with earth. They have known the sacred place in their own flesh, and nature takes on a new aspect. From now on they bear the name of Hadj, and nature is real because it is sanctified by their pilgrimage. The mystical union is accomplished, and they need no longer live in expectancy. To become master of the soil the pilgrim must cross the desert, so that reality is not transcended but mastered, so that nature ceases to be the constant temptation of the sacred.

The temple of Jerusalem never gave a fixed point to hope nor put an end to waiting. Jerusalem is the city of the marriage of man and space, to be accomplished only in the future; but the wait cannot be abandoned without loss of self, without inevitable exile and pilgrimage.

Rome is a consecration of the full stop; it is the acceptance of a nature that cannot be transcended while we are within it, of a city which is merely the stage where life is played, a place of transients (since real life cannot exist in space, in a fixed and visible location). Rome is the end of the long wait, it is resignation to the divorce of man from reality, the consummation of his separation; it is theatre triumphant.

Coming from the desert to the plenty of Europe, from absence to presence, the place was not for me a physical thing to be taken for granted, but a discovery and an acquisition. We cannot possess a place, but we can tame it in a transitory way. The choice is re-opened every moment. The place exists because it changes us; if it does not it is mere decor and we are in exile. The Orient, which denies the place, sanctifies it in compensation. Sanctification is a victory over exile, and I learned this on the shores of the West, where nature could be neither a decor nor a stopover. I learned to sanctify place to make it livable, but to my surprise it grew habitable independently of me, offering its blessings, its wealth, its beauties and colours, generously and of its own accord. Yet this autonomy of place can send me back into exile as easily as any hostility or desolation of place. I have to earn my own locale, I must win my home and merit it. If a change of place is not to be merely an exchange of one kind of exile for another, I must inhabit my home fully, make every minute sacred. This real link with place is the living experience that conducts us to the sacred. I am present at the creation of the world, but am not and cannot be a mere spectator. The world is not a theatre, I am participating in its creation. This is the poetic act, but it is also the negation of poetry. The conquest of each moment, the creation of place, is the living experience called poetry, a continuous invention; and yet by the same token any expression of the moment, of the sacred, becomes empty, exhausted in the very process of consummation.

I change cities. One succeeds the other, not superimposed but contesting one another. If I resist the temptation of exile it is at the price of comfort, external harmony, any obvious concord. My habitation is in dispute, and I occupy tensions which must each day be overcome; each day I must admit that the place has no reality unless I create it at every moment. I can no longer enjoy a relaxed and innocent rapport, from the moment a new place puts the first in question. And the new place itself is challenged, for now I must live in it with my eyes open. I choose it, and must constantly rebuild and reconsitute it. Otherwise the challenges drive me to escapism, to the refuge of exile, or to the annihilation of the real place by the absence of all links between us.

I have known the desert and the great wastes of snow, and for me the desert and the snowy wastes have forever lost their innocence.

I belong to a contested minority. I have lived in the shadow of great civilisations. Some were falling apart, others were in the throes of creation, founding themselves on disagreement with that relationship to reality which my minority has never wholly achieved, but which it has always persisted in pursuing. My minority, in spite of itself, has become a reminder and a hope.

Islam rode through the world bearing witness with the sword and the word. It accepted the survival in its midst of a different vision of hope, that of the Jews: a vision well-developed and vibrant enough to open the possibility of a challenge, but too feeble for the challenge to be real or do more than confirm the majority in its rights and certainties.

At the end of my adolescence, on the threshold of manhood, I discovered Christianity. I could at any time have protected my contested humanity by clothing myself in this foreign exoticism. I also knew the Arab minority, one not unlike my own, which lived first as a challenge to Christianity and then defensively, searching for inner strength with which to combat the western attempt to still its feeble, persistent voice, its reminder, plaintive but insistent and indomitable, of a lack, a non-achievement, an absence. I was able to compare Islam with Christianity only on the basis of the relation each has with Judaism, which has itself become a private consciousness, and an unhappy one. Here again I found myself in a minority, but this time on my own terms, for I was twice outnumbered: once by Christianity and again by western Judaism, which has perhaps not changed its attitude of expectancy, but has indeed changed its dream, giving a different resonance to its will, a different colour to its obstinacy.

Thus the West opposed me doubly and exercised a double temptation: to lose myself in a despised minority, or simply to lose myself. Then came the long apprenticeship of a strange language and the weight of unfamiliar words; and then, the discovery of relationships with humans, suddenly fully present for me because of my need to take note of them, if only in profile.

As a child, speaking to the Moslems of my own city, in their dialect rather than my own, I had a forewarning of what it was to belong to a minority, and I refused to accept that condition. I had to give way to the majority, hide the light of my way of speech, and adopt that of others in order to come closer to them, speaking to them on their terms, willing to forego the need for equality, as one must in any true exchange. My faith was my secret, and a secret need only be shameful for it to become a shackle.

Finally I refused to hide my origin and reject my dialect. I did not want my relationship with the majority to be established at the expense of the idea I had of myself. The more this idea became conscious, the more decisive it was for me. Gradually this lucid awareness seemed to me a privilege, and my weakness became a strength. The one who addressed me knew that I was different, that I was the foreigner. But I not only knew that he was the Other, I also knew that he saw in me the foreigner. This was the advantage I had over him: an indirect rapport that was consciously doubled back. Would he oblige me to play the role he had assigned to me? This is where the Orient I carry in me comes to the surface, and acquires the weight of consciousness. Western man has been schooled by his theatre. For centuries he has been perfecting the division of his personality. Between him and the one who addressed him, dialogue was at first established tortuously. The member of a minority had to accept his condition and recognise the privileged position of the other by adopting his way of speech. After centuries of conceptualisation it was easy to raise a screen between speakers, to separate them from their origins, until each came to consider himself as member of a majority, taking care to meet the Other only on neutral ground where each could maintain the idea he had of himself, revealing to the other only a facade. Theatre became the neutral ground where each man accepted the death of his self in the presence of others, in order that he might keep the secret which was his breath of life.

Politeness became a safe-conduct for crossing the zone that separated reality from theatre. There was no need to change facial expressions, for the real face was masked. Dissimulation became quite unconscious. It was merely one aspect of the theatre that pervaded and replaced life.

I was used to greater frankness, but also to a real dissimulation. In the Orient, because the rapport between man and reality is not theatrical, one looks for relationships that are direct and not oblique, though in full awareness that they are unattainable. And when one has recourse to theatre, it is not as a system on which to base a world-view but as a mechanism, a subterfuge, an instrument that must be spontaneously invented. If passions, despite their violence, seem ephemeral in the Orient, it is because they are not confined within a system of mediation which would formalise them and rob them of their spontaneity (while constantly feeding them). In the Orient passions succeed each other, like fidelities, and renew themselves. Though they may lack constancy they do not lose their reality. There may be dissimulation, but each face keeps its character and becomes its living self again at the first opportunity. It dons successive states. It is multiple, unpredictable. One cannot rely on any theatrical consistency, for this face is touched at every moment by the movement of life, a movement that is unpredictable and uncontrollable.

My self-division in the Orient was a ruse borrowed by passion for its own survival. The face changes colour so as not to go inert. This changing face that refuses the mask of death in fact makes death draw back. Speaking the Moslems' dialect, I merely muted one passion in order to participate in another—but now on my own conditions. And I always ended up deep in the game, for all consciousness would have been impotent if the motor of my behaviour had been a concentration on the immobility of death, rather than life in its iridescence.

In the West I discovered politeness and lucidity. I discovered theatre. Here self-division was not a succession of facial expressions; it was more basic. It affected my relationships with others and my rapport with reality. What for me had been a game, an improvisation, spontaneity, became a system, an instrument of survival. What had been freedom and a ruse of life became an enslavement, self-abandonment, resignation to death. I knew now that my Eastern theatre in occidental eyes meant duplicity and hypocrisy, that what was transitory was seen as frivolity. The iridescence of life was here suspect.

I changed my language and my vision of reality was overturned. Then suddenly in some oriental restaurant, I would hear a recording of Arab music and the forgotten world was there again, for an instant as well-defined and terminal as parentheses. What had been a natural part of life became a dream, a contrived atmosphere. At any cost I had to avoid the trap of homesickness, to save what for me remained my true rapport with reality. Then there was the little group of compatriots whom I could isolate and abstract from the world around. With them I would speak my own language avidly, with the pleasure of a lost gift recovered, a skill buried and found again. But this was yielding to the temptations of exile; and were not homesickness and exile precisely the theatre the Orient could not accept without denying itself and dying inwardly—the theatre the West had systematised so well?

I had to make the attempt to guard the Orient from exile and homesickness, but without artificial distractions. It was a rescue operation, but the rapport with reality that was to be rescued had not yet been established. It was still in the realm of desire. And in any case direct rapport with reality had to be lived in its own locale. Transplanted, it became theatre. I found myself plunging headfirst into the dilemma: recapture the Orient and protect myself from western theatre; yet also experience the West completely without embracing its divisions and dichotomies. Two ways were open to me. I could try to transform the West, approach it on my own terms, as if it were new and made no stipulations. But this was too ambitious; it overestimated my strength and underestimated the true dimensions of the West. Or I could lodge the Orient within me, make it a personal realm, neither dream nor illusion but a private place where the rapport with reality could become an immediate presence, a disposition to spontaneity. In other words, the Orient could become the domain of poetry. What was no longer open to me in daily life might be possible in moments of heightened intensity.

But daily life has its own power. I move among beings whose life is single, unique as it may be. I envy them, while pitying their poverty. My own life is twofold, or can be. But at what a price! I know that I am different and the others know I am conscious of my difference. This game of "I know that you know that I know" can be prolonged indefinitely, precisely because it is a game. To be foreign and conscious of it in no way diminishes the anguish of absence. The great dilemma is to be present and to accept being different.

Are we not all *marranos*?[1] At some point in our lives we carefully hide the thing that gives our existence its very weight and substance. We shield our secret from hostile eyes. And we are ashamed of it. Exile is a refuge, a safe harbour that allows us to practise virtue in a world busy erasing it. Exile could be sweet if it were no more than the tribute I pay a hostile world, one that forces me to live in pretended harmony with reality. Yet refusing exile, obliged to lead a diminished life, I am no less concerned about substance and reality. I talk to those around me and it is an act of rescue: these shadows in a weightless world are lit up by my concern. A part of myself becomes theirs, and already we are in communion. Their world is mine. They grasp this fact. What perturbation have I brought into these lives, that never before questioned their own validity? My tensions become theirs, and now it is they who prefer exile, taking refuge in their certainties. I violate their quiet, I overturn their private worlds. I am no longer the foreigner but the intruder. What a temptation now to retreat to the warmth of my own ghetto! My exile would become attractive, I could endow it with all the attributes of autonomy, I could have a separate life and the illusion of a full one. No one chooses tension cavalierly, and it is the need for peace and the warmth of certainties that drive the foreigner to become a *marrano*. How can I abandon my certainties without shaking those of others? One cannot exchange a set of certainties for another without living in a shadow universe. But I can become a *marrano* only as a last resort, out of my own cowardice or that of others. Then I will pretend to share the certainties of the new society while jealously safeguarding my own. I will accept a world of unreal appearance. Theatre is at work, and sets up its screen between myself and others when I need and seek a link with them. The breath of life becomes a secret cult, presence and absence are blurred, and death has the upper hand.

I must crack the walls protecting others, make them realise that they too are strangers, foreigners, arouse doubt where there was certainty, make complacent men admit that the foreigner is not merely the Other, the one who has come from another place, and that their own place can change its nature through the presence of the stranger if he is not pushed back into sham and pretence, if he himself does not accept the notion of exile. Only in this way can I overcome the condition of *marrano*. To those I trust, I open the strangeness and novelty of natural place, for I confer upon it the sacred character of presence. And we succeed together in living certain privileged moments, brief, dangerous, exacting, and forbidding. Suddenly reality seems not to be a certainty but something that must be won through an incessant struggle. We succeed only by living two lives. We know, if only unconsciously, that these moments of freedom and abandon, these extensions of all our individual lives into those of others, will be followed by long hours in which we will be alone and will have to prepare a place for our solitudes; hours when the paths of exile, relativity, and absence will lie before us as constant temptations. We will have to pass through the strait gate — the waiting and ancient hope — while realising that we all lead double lives, and that, if we persist in rejecting the theatrical, we must resign ourselves to being torn by our inner division. One moment I am with others; in the next, I am the stranger to them. In rhythmic alternation we are close, then strangers, and in this balancing act our equilibrium is re-established; our rapport with reality is not theatrical because we turn our backs on exile and *marranism*. The distance that rules each of my gestures toward the Other does not separate me from him, for it is born continually of alternation. If I accept the fact of being divided between communion and the ancient hope, it is because I reject the division of being, I refuse to live simultaneously in two worlds. My two universes are not superimposed. They continue each other, prolong one another in the movement that is life. Though my relationship with reality is conscious, it is not frozen by a lucidity of awareness that rules out adventure or chance. Alternation within continuity is creation; and my rapport with others is not a closed achievement but an eternal starting-point. I have opted for a language which I must invent as I speak. I have chosen a place which I endow with presence by inscribing my invention upon it. I have chosen a rapport with others which, far from imprisoning them in their own language or in a fixed place not of their choosing, draws them into a movement where language, place and the Other are invented every moment, obliging me to invent myself. I do not accept the fixity of safe places or the comfort of certitudes.

NORTHROP FRYE

The Motive for Metaphor

FOR THE PAST TWENTY-FIVE YEARS I have been teaching and studying English literature in a university. As in any other job, certain questions stick in one's mind, not because people keep asking them, but because they're the questions inspired by the very fact of being in such a place. What good is the study of literature? Does it help us to think more clearly, or feel more sensitively, or live a better life than we could without it? What is the function of the teacher and scholar, or of the person who calls himself, as I do, a literary critic? What difference does the study of literature make in our social or political or religious attitude? In my early days I thought very little about such questions, not because I had any of the answers, but because I assumed that anybody who asked them was naïve. I think now that the simplest questions are not only the hardest to answer, but the most important to ask, so I'm going to raise them and try to suggest what my present answers are. I say try to suggest, because there are only more or less inadequate answers to such questions — there aren't any right answers. The kind of problem that literature raises is not the kind that you ever "solve". Whether my answers are any good or not, they represent a fair amount of thinking about the questions. As I can't see my audience, I have to choose my rhetorical style in the dark, and I'm taking the classroom style, because an audience of students is the one I feel easiest with.

There are two things in particular that I want to discuss with you.

In school, and in university, there's a subject called "English" in English-speaking countries. English means, in the first place, the mother tongue. As that, it's the most practical subject in the world: you can't understand anything or take any part in your society without it. Wherever illiteracy is a problem, it's as fundamental a problem as getting enough to eat or a place to sleep. The native language takes precedence over every other subject of study: nothing else can compare with it in its usefulness. But then you find that every mother tongue, in any developed or civilized society, turns into something called literature. It you keep on studying "English", you find yourself trying to read Shakespeare and Milton. Literature, we're told, is one of the arts, along with painting and music, and, after you've looked up all the hard words and the Classical allusions and learned what words like imagery and diction are supposed to mean, what you use in understanding it, or so you're told, is your imagination. Here you don't seem to be in quite the same practical and useful area: Shakespeare and Milton, whatever their merits, are not the kind of thing you must know to hold any place in society at all. A person who knows nothing about literature may be an ignoramus, but many people don't mind being that. Every child realizes that literature is taking him in a different direction from the immediately useful, and a good many children complain loudly about this. Two questions I want to deal with, then, are, first: what is the relation of English as the mother tongue to English as a literature? Second: What is the social value of the study of literature, and what is the place of the imagination that literature addresses itself to, in the learning process?

Let's start with the different ways there are of dealing with the world we're living in. Suppose you're shipwrecked on an uninhabited island in the South Seas. The first thing you do is to take a long look at the world around you, a world of sky and sea and earth and stars and trees and hills. You see this world as objective, as something set over against you and not yourself or related to you in any way. And you notice two things about this objective world. In the first place, it doesn't have any conversation. It's full of animals and plants and insects going on with their own business, but there's nothing that responds to you: it has no morals and no intelligence, or at least none that you can grasp. It may have a shape and a meaning, but it doesn't seem to be a human shape or a human meaning. Even if there's enough to eat and no dangerous animals, you feel lonely and frightened and unwanted in such a world.

In the second place, you find that looking at the world, as something set over against you, splits your mind in two. You have an intellect that feels curious about it and wants to study it, and you have feelings or emotions that see it as beautiful or austere or terrible. You know that both these attitudes have some reality, at least for you. If the ship you were wrecked in was a Western ship, you'd probably feel that your intellect tells you more about what's really there in the outer world, and that your emotions tell you more about what's going on inside you. If your background were Oriental, you'd be more likely to reverse this and say that the beauty or terror was what was really there, and that your instinct to count and classify and measure and pull to pieces was what was inside your mind. But whether your point of view is Western or Eastern, intellect and emotion never get together in your mind as long as you're simply looking at the world. They alternate, and keep you divided between them.

The language you use on this level of the mind is the language of consciousness or awareness. It's largely a language of nouns and adjectives. You have to have names for things, and you need qualities like "wet" or "green" or "beautiful" to describe how things seem to you. This is the speculative or contemplative position of the mind, the position in which the arts and sciences begin, although they don't stay there very long. The sciences begin by accepting the facts and the evidence about an outside world without trying to alter them. Science proceeds by accurate measurement and description, and follows the demands of the reason rather than the emotions. What it deals with is there, whether we like it or not. The emotions are unreasonable: for them it's what they like and don't like that comes first. We'd be naturally inclined to think that the arts follow the path of emotion, in contrast to the sciences. Up to a point they do, but there's a complicating factor.

That complicating factor is the contrast between "I like this" and "I don't like this". In this Robinson Crusoe life I've assigned you, you may have moods of complete peacefulness and joy, moods when you accept your island and everything around you. You wouldn't have such moods very often, and when you had them, they'd be moods of identification, when you felt that the island was a part of you and you a part of it. That is not the feeling of consciousness or awareness, where you feel split off from everything that's not your perceiving self. Your habitual state of mind is the feeling of separation which goes with being conscious, and the feeling "this is not a part of me" soon becomes "this is not what I want". Notice the word "want": we'll be coming back to it.

So you soon realize that there's a difference between the world you're living in and the world you want to live in. The world you want to live in is a human world, not an objective one: it's not an environment but a home; it's not the world you see but the world you build out of what you see. You go to work to build a shelter or plant a garden, and as soon as you start to work you've moved into a different level of human life. You're not separating only yourself from nature now, but constructing a human world and separating it from the rest of the world. Your intellect and emotions are now both engaged in the same activity, so there's no longer any real distinction between them. As soon as you plant a garden or a crop, you develop the conception of a "weed", the plant you don't want in there. But you can't say that "weed" is either an intellectual or an emotional conception, because it's both at once. Further, you go to work because you feel you have to, and because you want something at the end of the work. That means that the important categories of your life are no longer the subject and the object, the watcher and the things being watched: the important categories are what you have to do and what you want to do — in other words, necessity and freedom.

One person by himself is not a complete human being, so I'll provide you with another shipwrecked refugee of the opposite sex and an eventual family. Now you're a member of a human society. This human society after a while will transform the island into something with a human shape. What that human shape is, is revealed in the shape of the work you do: the buildings, such as they are, the paths through the woods, the planted crops fenced off against whatever animals want to eat them. These things, these rudiments of city, highway, garden, and farm, are the human form of nature, or the form of human nature, whichever you like. This is the area of the applied arts and sciences, and it appears in our society as engineering and agriculture and medicine and architecture. In this area we can never say clearly where the art stops and the science begins, or vice versa.

The language you use on this level is the language of practical sense, a language of verbs or words of action and movement. The practical world, however, is a world where actions speak louder than words. In some way it's a higher level of existence than the speculative level, because it's doing something about the world instead of just looking at it, but in itself it's a much more primitive level. It's the process of adapting to the environment, or rather of transforming the environment in the interests of one species, that goes on among animals and plants as well as human beings. The animals have a good many of our practical skills: some insects make pretty fair architects, and beavers know quite a lot about engineering. In this island, probably, and certainly if you were alone, you'd have about the ranking of a second-rate animal. What makes our practical life really human is a third level of the mind, a level where consciousness and practical skill come together.

This third level is a vision or model in your mind of what you want to construct. There's that word "want" again. The actions of man are prompted by desire, and some of these desires are needs, like food and warmth and shelter. One of these needs is sexual, the desire to reproduce and bring more human beings into existence. But there's also a desire to bring a social human form into existence: the form of cities and gardens and farms that we call civilization. Many animals and insects have this social form too, but man knows that he has it: he can compare what he does with what he can imagine being done. So we begin to see where the imagination belongs in the scheme of human affairs. It's the power of constructing possible models of human experience. In the world of the imagination, anything goes that's imaginatively possible, but nothing really happens. If it did happen, it would move out of the world of imagination into the world of action.

We have three levels of the mind now, and a language for each of them, which in English-speaking societies means an English for each of them. There's the level of consciousness and awareness, where the most important thing is the difference between me and everything else. The English of this level is the English of ordinary conversation, which is mostly monologue, as you'll soon realize if you do a bit of eavesdropping, or listening to yourself. We can call it the language of self-expression. Then there's the level of social participation, the working or technological language of teachers and preachers and politicians and advertisers and lawyers and journalists and scientists. We've already called this the language of practical sense. Then there's the level of imagination, which produces the literary language of poems and plays and novels. They're not really different languages, of course, but three different reasons for using words.

On this basis, perhaps, we can distinguish the arts from the sciences. Science begins with the world we have to live in, accepting its data and trying to explain its laws. From there, it moves towards the imagination: it becomes a mental construct, a model of a possible way of interpreting experience. The further it goes in this direction, the more it tends to speak the language of mathematics, which is really one of the languages of the imagination, along with literature and music. Art, on the other hand, begins with the world we construct, not with the world we see. It starts with the imagination, and then works towards ordinary experience: that is, it tries to make itself as convincing and recognizable as it can. You can see why we tend to think of the sciences as intellectual and the arts as emotional: one starts with the world as it is, the other with the world we want to have. Up to a point it is true that science gives an intellectual view of reality, and that the arts try to make the emotions as precise and disciplined as sciences do the intellect. But of course it's nonsense to think of the scientist as a cold unemotional reasoner and the artist as somebody who's in a perpetual emotional tizzy. You can't distinguish the arts from the sciences by the mental processes the people in them use: they both operate on a mixture of hunch and common sense. A highly developed science and and a highly developed art are very close together, psychologically and otherwise.

Still, the fact that they start from opposite ends, even if they do meet in the middle, makes for one important difference between them. Science learns more and more about the world as it goes on: it evolves and improves. A physicist today knows more physics than Newton did, even if he's not as great a scientist. But literature begins with the possible model of experience, and what it produces is the literary model we call the classic. Literature doesn't evolve or improve or progress. We may have dramatists in the future who will write plays as good as *King Lear,* though they'll be very different ones, but drama as a whole will never get better than *King Lear. King Lear* is it, as far as drama is concerned; so is *Oedipus Rex,* written two thousand years earlier than that, and both will be models of dramatic writing as long as the human race endures. Social conditions may improve: most of us would rather live in nineteenth-century United States than in thirteenth-century Italy, and for most of us Whitman's celebration of democracy makes a lot more sense than Dante's Inferno. But it doesn't follow that Whitman is a better poet than Dante: literature won't line up with that kind of improvement.

So we find that everything that does improve, including science, leaves the literary artist out in the cold. Writers don't seem to benefit much by the advance of science, although they thrive on superstitions of all kinds. And you certainly wouldn't turn to contemporary poets for guidance or leadership in the twentieth-century world. You'd hardly go to Ezra Pound, with his facism and social credit and Confucianism and anti-semitism. Or to Yeats, with his spiritualism and fairies and astrology. Or to D. H. Lawrence, who'll tell you that it's a good thing for servants to be flogged because that restores the precious current of blood-reciprocity between servant and master. Or to T. S. Eliot, who'll tell you that to have a flourishing culture we should educate an élite, keep most people living in the same spot, and never disestab-

lish the Church of England. The novelists seem to be a little closer
to the world they're living in, but not much. When Communists
talk about the decadence of bourgeois culture, this is the kind of
thing they always bring up. Their own writers don't seem to be any
better, though; just duller. So the real question is a bigger one. Is it
possible that literature, especially poetry, is something that a
scientific civilization like ours will eventually outgrow? Man has
always wanted to fly, and thousands of years ago he was making
sculptures of winged bulls and telling stories about people who
flew so high on artificial wings that the sun melted them off. In an
Indian play fifteen hundred years old, *Sakuntala,* there's a god
who flies around in a chariot that to a modern reader sounds very
much like a private aeroplane. Interesting that the writer had so
much imagination, but do we need such stories now that we have
private aeroplanes?

This is not a new question: it was raised a hundred and fifty years
ago by Thomas Love Peacock, who was a poet and novelist
himself, and a very brilliant one. He wrote an essay called *Four
Ages of Poetry,* with his tongue of course in his cheek, in which he
said that poetry was the mental rattle that awakened the imagination of mankind in its infancy, but that now, in an age of science
and technology, the poet has outlived his social function. "A poet
in our times," said Peacock, "is a semi-barbarian in a civilized
community. He lives in the days that are past. His ideas, thoughts,
feelings, associations, are all with barbarous manners, obsolete
customs, and exploded superstitions. The march of his intellect is
like that of a crab, backwards." Peacock's essay annoyed his
friend Shelley, who wrote another essay called *A Defence of
Poetry* to refute it. Shelley's essay is a wonderful piece of writing,
but it's not likely to convince anyone who needs convincing. I
shall be spending a good deal of my time on this question of the
relevance of literature in the world of today, and I can only indicate
the general lines my answer will take. There are two points I can
make now, one simple, the other more difficult.

The simple point is that literature belongs to the world man
constructs, not to the world he sees; to his home, not his environment. Literature's world is a concrete human world of immediate

experience. The poet uses images and objects and sensations much
more than he uses abstract ideas; the novelist is concerned with
telling stories, not with working out arguments. The world of
literature is human in shape, a world where the sun rises in the east
and sets in the west over the edge of a flat earth in three dimensions, where the primary realities are not atoms or electrons but
bodies, and the primary forces not energy or gravitation but love
and death and passion and joy. It's not surprising if writers are
often rather simple people, not always what we think of as intellectuals, and certainly not always any freer of silliness or perversity
than anyone else. What concerns us is what they produce, not what
they are, and poetry, according to Milton, who ought to have
known, is "more simple, sensuous and passionate" than philosophy or science.

The more difficult point takes us back to what we said when we
were on that South Sea island. Our emotional reaction to the world
varies from "I like this" to "I don't like this". The first, we said,
was a state of identity, a feeling that everything around us was part
of us, and the second is the ordinary state of consciousness, or
separation, where art and science begin. Art begins as soon as "I
don't like this" turns into "this is not the way I could imagine it".
We notice in passing that the creative and the neurotic minds have
a lot in common. They're both dissatisified with what they see;
they both believe that something else ought to be there, and they
try to pretend it is there or to make it be there. The differences are
more important, but we're not ready for them yet.

At the level of ordinary consciousness the individual man is the
centre of everything, surrounded on all sides by what he isn't. At
the level of practical sense, or civilization, there's a human cir-
cumference, a little cultivated world with a human shape, fenced
off from the jungle and inside the sea and the sky. But in the
imagination anything goes that can be imagined, and the limit of
the imagination is a totally human world. Here we recapture, in
full consciousness, that original lost sense of identity with our
surroundings, where there is nothing outside the mind of man, or
something identical with the mind of man. Religions present us
with visions of eternal and infinite heavens or paradises which

have the form of the cities and gardens of human civilization, like
the Jerusalem and Eden of the Bible, completely separated from
the state of frustration and misery that bulks so large in ordinary
life. We're not concerned with these visions as religion, but they
indicate what the limits of the imagination are. They indicate too
that in the human world the imagination has no limits, if you
follow me. We said that the desire to fly produced the aeroplane.
But people don't get into planes because they want to fly; they get
into planes because they want to get somewhere else faster. What's
produced the aeroplane is not so much a desire to fly as a rebellion
against the tyranny of time and space. And that's a process that can
never stop, no matter how high our Titovs and Glenns may go.

   For each of these six talks I've taken a title from some work of
literature, and my title for this one is "The Motive for Metaphor",
from a poem of Wallace Stevens. Here's the poem:

> You like it under the trees in autumn,
> Because everything is half dead.
> The wind moves like a cripple among the leaves
> And repeats words without meaning.
>
> In the same way, you were happy in spring,
> With the half colors of quarter-things,
> The slightly brighter sky, the melting clouds,
> The single bird, the obscure moon —
>
> The obscure moon lighting an obscure world
> Of things that would never be quite expressed,
> Where you yourself were never quite yourself
> And did not want nor have to be,
>
> Desiring the exhilarations of changes:
> The motive for metaphor, shrinking from
> The weight of primary noon,
> The A B C of being,
>
> The ruddy temper, the hammer
> Of red and blue, the hard sound —
> Steel against intimation — the sharp flash,
> The vital, arrogant, fatal, dominant X.

What Stevens calls the weight of primary noon, the A B C of being, and the dominant X is the objective world, the world set over against us. Outside literature, the main motive for writing is to describe this world. But literature itself uses language in a way which associates our minds with it. As soon as you use associative language, you begin using figures of speech. If you say this talk is dry and dull, you're using figures associating it with bread and breadknives. There are two main kinds of association, analogy and identity, two things that are like each other and two things that are each other. You can say with Burns, "My love's like a red, red rose", or you can say with Shakespeare:

> Thou that art now the world's fresh ornament
> And only herald to the gaudy spring.

One produces the figure of speech called the simile; the other produces the figure called metaphor.

In descriptive writing you have to be careful of associative language. You'll find that analogy, or likeness to something else, is very tricky to handle in description, because the differences are as important as the resemblances. As for metaphor, where you're really saying "this *is* that", you're turning your back on logic and reason completely, because logically two things can never be the same thing and still remain two things. The poet, however, uses these two crude, primitive, archaic forms of thought in the most uninhibited way, because his job is not to describe nature, but to show you a world completely absorbed and possessed by the human mind. So he produces what Baudelaire called a "suggestive magic including at the same time object and subject, the world outside the artist and the artist himself". The motive for metaphor, according to Wallace Stevens, is a desire to associate, and finally to indentify, the human mind with what goes on outside it, because the only genuine joy you can have is in those rare moments when you feel that although we may know in part, as Paul says, we are also a part of what we know.

FREDELLE BRUSER MAYNARD

The Windless World

I REMEMBER THE DOG. He was a Spitz, I think, or a mongrel with a Spitzy tail, and he balanced on his hind legs on the cover of the Canadian Primer. There was an old woman, too — I learned afterwards that she was Mother Goose—contained, like the dog, within a sharp black circle. The angle of the old lady's scarf, blown forward with stiffly outthrust fringe, suggested wind, but the world of the figures was windless. The blackish, olive-tinted sky seemed absolutely serene; the meadow flowers, each separate on its tuft of careful grass, were still and perfect as the matching flowers on Mother Goose's gown. What was she saying, her pointing finger outlined against the sculptured scarf? Surely nothing so insipid as "Bow-wow-wow, whose dog art thou?" Momentous as an Egyptian hieroglyph on the door of an unopened tomb, the picture haunted me through all the hours in prairie schoolrooms. It mingled with the smell of chalk dust and eraser crumbs, of crude ink splashed into inkwells by unsteady jug-bearers, of apples and pencil shavings and gum. Perhaps it was only when I left the Canadian Readers, in grade six, that I knew for sure the message frozen on those parted lips. The voice of the reader was the voice of the Union Jack: Be Brave (red); Be Pure (white); Be True Blue.

Every autumn, after Labor Day, we got a new book. What a moment that was, the crisp stacks of readers lined up at the head of each row as we sat in the approved position, eyes front, hands folded, waiting for the signal: "Take one and pass them back." The sour green binding looked unpromising enough. After Books I and II, with their cover pictures, the Nelson Publishing Company made no further concessions to frivolity. Books III, IV, and V presented a uniform front, a Canadian coat of arms with the lion, the unicorn, and the fought-for crown poised above a shaky maple leaf spray. *A mari usque ad mare*, the banner read. From sea to sea, from September to September, the contents of those books were imprinted on the minds of young Canadians. In the small towns where I lived, there was little competition from other influences. We had no library, no magazine stands (or comic books); the radio was dominated by sopranos and the phonograph required cranking. So I read the readers. All through the years, I have remembered the thrilling stories of Horatius and Robin Hood. Fragments of verses, memorized long ago for the school inspector's visit, have blown about the borders of adult consciousness. "Let me live in a house by the side of the road/And be a friend to man." "Those behind cried 'Forward!' and those before cried 'Back!'" Were the Canadian Readers so rich as in retrospect they seemed? I often wondered. And then, in the musty basement of a Winnipeg bookstore, I found them—a full glorious set, Books I to V. Magic casements opening on the foam by faery seas — or windows on a petrified forest? I could scarcely wait to know.

I have gone all through the Canadian Readers now, starting with "Tom Tinker had a dog" and ending with Kipling's *Recessional*. A strange journey. A journey in search of myself, perhaps, but even more in search of the attitudes which molded my generation, and of a long since vanished world. It is easy to criticize the readers. What an extraordinary list of authors, for example: there is no Milton, no Shakespeare except for a snippet from *Julius Caesar* and a scene from *As You Like It*. There is not one song from Blake or Burns or Walter de la Mare. Longfellow, however, is most plentifully represented; so is James Whitcomb Riley. Much of the material is anonymous — for reasons which to the mature judgment seem clear. Imperialists abound. Kipling, Edward Shirley, Sir Henry Newbolt, Canon F. G. Scott blow their bugles mightily.

> Children of the Empire, you are brothers all;
> Children of the Empire, answer to the call;
> Let your voices mingle, lift your heads and sing;
> "God save dear old Britain, and God save Britain's king."

And behind them — a formidable array — march battalions of female poets with resonant triple names: Hannah Flagg Gould, Agnes Maule Machar, Julia Augusta Schwarz. Looking now at "The Crocus's Song" and "Christmas" ("Every mile is as warm as a smile, And every hour is a song") I can understand why I thought, as a child, that poetry must be easy to write.

In prose too, the style of the readers offers some melancholy models. " 'Let me get up,' said I, waxing wroth, for reasons I cannot tell you, because they are too manifold." Events are hung in mists of sentimental vagueness. The child who longs to *see* the guests at Allan-a-Dale's wedding is told only that "there were a great many lovely ladies in beautiful dresses". Why was Father Valentine beloved? Because he told "wonderful stories" and taught "beautiful things". When not teaching beautiful things, he sat in his room writing "the kind words which had always made his visits so full of good cheer". What would a third-grader make of the bare statement (in "Pippa") that "A great deed that the world needed must be done, and the man loved the great deed"? How would a fifth-grader respond to Lord Avebury's solemn advice: "Time spent in innocent and rational enjoyments, in healthy games, in social and family intercourse, is well and wisely spent"? From diversions like this, a young scholar must have skipped lightly home to the chores.

Illustrations for the Canadian Readers include a good deal of amateurish line drawing, dark blurred photographs, and acres of third-rate academy painting. Sometimes the pictures bear directly on the text, sometimes they are just vaguely related in feeling, as when "Dog of Flanders", about a boy and his dog, is introduced by the painting of a girl and her sheep. Landscape studies predominate, but it is a landscape startingly irrelevant to the experience of the audience. Apart from some amusing "oriental" scenes, the world of the readers is English: indoors, nannies and beautifully groomed children at teatime; outdoors, a fairyland of stone walls and hawthorns where blackbirds sing from the blooming apple boughs. To the child who rode to school on horseback, past sloughs and wheatfields and elevators, the visions of Rosa Bonheur must have been outlandish as Aladdin.

In addition to being remote, the world of the readers is limited. An adult today is struck by a peculiarly English class consciousness. For example, the account of a rogue named Greene, who led the mutiny against Henry Hudson, begins with a raised-monocle observation to the effect that "this Greene was of respectable connections". Not surprisingly, it's a man's world. The few women celebrated are those who prove themselves in war the equal of men — Boadicea, Laura Secord, Florence Nightingdale, Edith Cavell. (There is one essay called "A Pioneer Woman", but the achievements of its heroine are a sad anticlimax. "Mrs. Lajimodière was not, of course, expected to carry a load or to use a paddle, but the journey from Montreal to Pembina must have been one of great hardship to her. She had often to pass the whole day seated on the bottom of the canoe." We are not told whether she carried a parasol.) Even more serious is the indifference, through all five volumes, to people of other lands. There is the British Empire, and beyond that a wasteland inhabited by funny little people like Oogly the Eskimo and Ning Ting "away over in an eastern country called China". Japan is a place where "there isn't a sofa or chair", where one eats without a fork and rides in neat little rickshaws. You will find "in Japan that your horse is a man". Not surprising, I guess, to a child who, in the phonetic tables accompanying Book I, is given the series "nap, rap, gap, *Jap*". There are Indians in these stories, but not the Sioux or Cree of any Canadian's real experience. Gorgeously outfitted in buckskin, they sit under giant oaks whispering their secrets to squirrels. They have never seen a reservation, and they have no embarrassing Problems.

Perhaps it is unfair to protest, in material for the primary grades, the absence of any scholarly or scientific spirit. Still, it does seem that the borders between real and fanciful might have been more clearly defined. In grade three the student learns how umbrellas were invented (an elf, threatened with a soaking, uproots a toadstool) and how James Watt discovered the principle of steam. He passes, without change in style or tone, from Robinson Crusoe to Lord Nelson. (I suspect that most little readers found Crusoe the more credible of the two.) Imaginary events are "proved" by the real existence of places named. Allan-a-Dale's marriage? "To this day you can still see the ruins of the great abbey in which it took place." The Pied Piper? "If you go to Hamelin, the people will show you the hill and the river." *Quod erat demonstrandum*. Even historical material is presented with a curious indifference to fact. Florence Nightingale is described as having personally cared for 10,000 sick. We are told how Sir Philip Sidney looked when he offered a dying soldier his last cup of water — but not the name of the "great battle" just fought. Did the teachers of the 1920s fill in the blanks, supply the necessary correctives? Perhaps some did. But in the one-room schools of my acquaintance the teacher, often fresh out of Normal School, was glad if she had time to hear us recite. Anything else was extra and impossible. I don't recall that a teacher ever provided us with the background, say, for the scene from *David Copperfield*, or played the music which was the subject of "The Moonlight Sonata" and with which we were all supposed to be "so fondly acquainted".

"The Moonlight Sonata" offers a shining instance of a Canadian Reader specialty: the sentimental scene. All the ingredients are here — poverty, affliction, simple virtue and the reward it brings. Beethoven, out for a midnight stroll, hears music and sobbing. Entering the "little, mean dwelling", he finds a pale young man making shoes and a blind girl bent over her harpsichord, dreaming hopelessly of the good music she has no opportunity to hear. Beethoven sits down at the instrument. Luckily, it is in perfect tune, or tunes up quickly at the master's touch. ("From the instant that his fingers began to wander along the keys, the very tone of the harpsichord began to grow sweeter and more equal.") Inspired by the young people's devotion — "they covered his hands with tears and kisses"—he improvises a sonata to the moonlight, then dashes home to record the music — not, however, without promising to give lessons to the young lady. (No biographer tells us how often he returned.) Another favorite tear-jerker was "The Lark at the Diggings". Listening to the song of the little brown bird, hardened criminals, exiled to Australia, are reduced to tears. Shaggy lips tremble as the song evokes visions of "the old mother's tears, when he left her without one grain of sorrow, the village church and its simple chimes" and "the chubby playmates that never grew to be wicked".

In order that our chubby childhood might be secure from temptation, the readers lectured us continually. "Teach us to bear the yoke in youth" was the burden of the inappropriately named "Children's Song". "Teach us to rule ourselves alway, Controlled and cleanly night and day." Goodness was a full-time job, *that* was clear. How we marveled at the story of David Livingstone, a perfect lad even before Africa beckoned. "When he swept the room for his mother, there was no leaving of dust in dark corners where it might not be noticed, no dusting round in circles and not underneath." At ten, this paragon earned his own living at a cotton mill: up at five, then fourteen hours at the loom, a Latin grammar (bought with his first earnings) propped at eye level. "It might have been supposed," ran the text, "that after fourteen hours at the factory, David would have been glad to rest or play when he got home at night." But no. Home from work, he hurried off to night school; home from night school, he pored over his books until Mother blew out the candle. Of course, "whenever there was a Missionary Meeting held within walking distance he was always there." At the looms, too, joining threads, "he began to weave his plan of service for his Master." And from all the grueling routine he emerged fresh as a sprig of Scots heather.

"Whenever a holiday came round he showed what a splendid out-of-door boy he was as well."

Few of us could have hoped to emulate this noble life—for one thing, cotton mills were scarce on the Canadian prairies—but we were given plenty of help. Poems, stories, biographies — all uplifted. There were tongues in the trees, books in the running brooks, sermons in stones, and Good in everything. Literally. What does the crocus say, deep in the snow?

> I will peer up with my bright little head
> I will peer up with my bright little head.

giving us a lesson to borrow, that

> Patient today, through its gloomiest hour
> We come out the brighter tomorrow.

Willows demonstrate helpfulness; rabbits, the rewards of unselfishness. Sunbeams discover that "in seeking the pleasures Of others [we've] filled to the full [our] own measure". Hens are punctual; bees, naturally, industrious; horses know how important it is to "Do your best wherever you are, and keep up your good name". If you listen carefully to the song the whitethroat sings, you will find that it is a patriot bird: "I-love-dear-Canada, Canada, Canada." Beavers are introduced early into the business of cutting trees for the winter, and you know what? "The little fellows found that work was even better fun than play." Over and over again, we are reminded that though intelligence and tender feeling are goods, there is one Good greater far. With the anonymous singer of Book IV, we cheerfully learn to say,

> Head, you may think; Heart, you may feel;
> But, Hand you shall work alway.

I can smile, now, at the naïve moralizing of the Canadian Readers. It did no harm; perhaps many children profited. But one aspect,

one direction, of the material still seems to me pernicious, unforgivable: the exaltation of empire and the glorification of war.
Through the whole five volumes, only two selections suggest in
any way the virtues of peace. One is about a statue of Christ erected
in the Andes, the other a rather pallid account of the League of
Nations. Drowning out these faint whispers, the drums of war beat
loud. This is a world where little boys dream of battle. ''I will try to
be very good,'' says Jackanapes, son of a father killed at Waterloo.
''But I should like to be a soldier.'' His grandfather's old heart
swells with pride. ''You shall, my boy, you shall.'' A tale of
powder-monkeys, for the third grade, describes the thrill of children on warships ''going about [their] work amid the smoke and
thunder of the guns, and seeing men struck down beside them by
the fire of the enemy''. A bit dangerous, of course, ''but it was a
fine training for the boys''. Some of them even become admirals,
and in this world making admiral is a big thing. Columbus was an
admiral. So was Sir Cloudesley Shovell and Grenville and Raleigh
and Drake.

> Admirals all, for England's sake . . .
> They left us a kingdom none can take,
> The realm of the circling sea.

If the kingdom must be won with human lives, that is a pity,
certainly. But the true Briton sees these things *sub specie aeternitatis*.

> Though our only reward be the thrust of a sword
> And a bullet in heart or brain,
> What matters one gone, if the flag float on,
> And Britain be Lord of the Main!

Four years after the close of the First World War, schoolchildren
are invited to admire a battle for the Yser Canal, ''an inferno of
destruction and death''. Shells burst, flames cloud the moon, and
the great guns roar. ''It was glorious,'' writes the author. ''It was

terrible. It was inspiring.'' Poet Laureate John Masefield describes the battle of Gallipoli in terms which emphasize, ultimately, its dreadful brilliance. Within hours, he speculates of a departing troop ship, one tenth of the men "would have looked their last on the sun, and be a part of foreign earth or dumb things that the tides push''. One third would be "mangled, blinded, or broken, lamed, made imbecile, or disfigured''; the rest would suffer agonies in the trenches. Still, the little readers are reminded ''these things were but the end they asked, the reward they had come for, the unseen cross upon the breast. All that they felt was a gladness of exultation that their young courage was to be used. They went like kings in a pageant to the imminent death.''

One can smile, now, at the Canadian Readers. Naïve, jingoistic, unscholarly, sentimental, moralistic — they were all these. And yet the fact remains that they were also memorable and moving. Few children of this generation will cherish their memories of Dick and Jane. But who could forget Jack Cornwall, the hero of the Battle of Jutland, or Madeleine, the heroine of Verchères? What are Spot and Puff compared with Bruin, the Canadian bear who terrorized a lumber camp, and gentle Patrasche, who pulled a milk cart for love? The world of the readers was a world of heroes. And in the end it didn't much matter, I think, that these heroes were dedicated to purposes which a modern finds questionable — the invincibility of the British fleet, or the glories of empire. What mattered greatly, to all of us who succumbed to its spell, was the vision of men committed to a principle beyond self. I think of Grace Darling, rowing out to a shipwreck through furious seas; of plucky little Pierre, who stole through the German lines to bring news that would save his village; of Captains Scott's last journey, and the dying Oates, who walked out into the blizzard to relieve others of responsibility for his care. In the end, the British Empire became a kind of metaphor — for honor, dignity, unselfishness, and courage. In today's schoolbooks, the captains and the kings depart — and what is left is the kid next door.

Along with the sense of the heroic the readers communicated

something equally valuable, a sense of the importance of the individual. Every man *mattered*. Any man might become great. Little Antonio, who carved a lion out of butter for a rich man's table, becomes a famous sculptor; honest Michael, an ordinary Dutch sailor, risks death rather than betray his master and rises "step by step till he became an admiral". Whatever stone you cast into the waters carried reverberations to distant shores. John Cornwall, mortally wounded but still manning a gun, wins "a renown that can never fade so long as men reverence . . . Duty and Honor". The story of Grace Darling's brave deed "was told all over Europe and America. High and low, rich and poor, united to sing her praises and extol her bravery." It is not true, I see now, that Alan McLeod, V.C., "left behind an undying story and an immortal name". (Who *was* Alan McLeod?) But I am glad that I grew up believing in such a possibility.

The vision of the Canadian Readers was limited; it focused almost exclusively on a Protestant, Anglo-Saxon ideal. But it was always a moral vision. Open a modern school anthology and you will be struck with its efficient treatment of man as a social being: here is the real world of real children working, playing, or, as the psychologists would say, interacting. Open the Canadian Readers and you will find an often passionate concentration on what makes a man *a man*. This is true from the very beginning. Consider, for example, the First Reader story of "The Little Blue Egg". A boy, a decent chap really, takes just one peep at the nest, and then — they are *so* pretty — just one egg. The bird will surely not miss it. But at night, the egg safely hidden, he cannot sleep. However deep he huddles into the bedclothes he hears at the window a voice louder than any bird: BRING BACK MY LITTLE BLUE EGG. Compare this with an episode from a modern grade one reader.

> Sally found a big white egg.
> "I will take this," she said.
> "It looks like a ball."

Her brother sets her straight.

> "You funny girl," laughed Dick.
> "I cannot play ball with that egg.
> You must take it to Grandmother."
> Away Sally ran to the house.

Sally has learned, I suppose, a useful lesson. An egg is an egg is not a ball. But it's a far cry from the deep moral shudder communicated by that long-ago tale of the fatal blue egg.

Instead of the familiar — in vocabulary, situation, and scene — the Canadian Readers confronted us constantly with the unfamiliar, the strange. It was not a bad idea. "Sleep, baby, sleep!" runs a poem in the primer. "The large stars are the sheep; The little stars are the lambs, I guess, The bright moon is the shepherdess. Sleep, baby, sleep." Any first-grade teacher knows that "shepherdess" is a hard word for six-year-olds — but how nice that we heard it so young. As for the unfamiliar scenery presented in the Academy paintings; we had all seen enough tractors, and one mile of prairie is much like another. The images of orchards and castle walls were not baffling but liberating; they gave us room to grow.

A final observation about the Canadian Readers. Theirs was a world of extraordinary security and joy. The pages shine with birds and stars and flowers. What does the thrush say, little girl, little boy?

> O, the world's running over with joy!
> Don't you hear? don't you see?
> Hush! look here! in my tree
> I am as happy as happy can be.

Minutes later — another page, another poem — he is joined by the chickadee ("Good morning! Oh, who are as happy as we?") and, in "Spring Waking", by a redbreast.

A Robin began to sing,
The air grew warm, and the grass turned green.
"Spring!" laughed the Sun "'tis Spring!"

There are fields and fields of joyful flowers unfolding in the sun:

"Wake," said the sunshine, "and creep to the light."
"Wake," said the voice of the raindrops bright.
The little plant heard it, and rose to see
What the wonderful outside world might be.

When snow overwhelmed the prairies, blotting out the memory of green, how pleasant to be assured that March's call, "Ho there! Ho!" would be answered by "Ha! Ha! Ha!"

In a chorus soft and low
From the millions of flowers under the ground —
Yes — millions — beginning to grow.

In this best of all possible worlds, snow implied sunshine and rain, flowers. Darkness was an illusion.

'Tis always morning somewhere, and above
The awakening continents from shore to shore
Somewhere the birds are singing evermore.

Above all, it was a solid, comfortable, ordered universe, where evil was always vanquished and right enthroned.

Truth shall conquer at the last,
For round and round we run,
and ever the right comes uppermost,
And ever is justice done.

And what was truth? It was not various and shifting, but a standard clear to rational man. "Teach us," we sang in "Land of our Birth", "The Truth whereby the Nations live." *The Truth*, in capital letters—single, absolute, in all times and places infallible. Perhaps it is the sense which, in the end, makes the intellectual landscape of the readers remote as the Land of Oz. Chicken Little set out, in the primer, to tell the king the sky was falling, but we knew it was only a leaf. For this was indeed the windless world. How could we have guessed the sky would ever fall?

FRANK UNDERHILL
Goldwin Smith[1]

IT IS NOW twenty-three years since Goldwin Smith died. During his career, both in England and in Canada, he was engaged in almost continuous controversy; and during the last thirty-nine years of his life he resided in a city which, while it respected him highly for his attainments, abhorred his political views and never made much attempt to understand him. Though he had been a Regius Professor of History, his own writings were mostly in the nature of journalism, and they are already largely forgotten by Canadians, who, as inveterate newspaper readers, are a people with short memories. His secretary, Mr. Arnold Haultain, who was his literary executor, has left us the only attempt at a full-length portrait that we have; it was painted when Mr. Haultain was smarting a little from a sense of ill-treatment, and it shows much more concentration upon the warts than upon the rest of the face. Besides, no man was ever more completely unfitted by temperament for understanding the real elements of Goldwin Smith's greatness than was Mr. Haultain. He had a naive instinctive admiration for everything which his chief detested. He bubbled with enthusiasm for the Chamberlainite imperialism of the late 1890s and early 1900s, and he believed firmly that Rudyard Kipling was a poet.

It seems, therefore, worth while, even though the issue between Cobden and Chamberlain is not yet settled in the British Empire, to survey afresh the development of Goldwin Smith's ideas. The more difficult task of estimating his influence in Canada I shall not attempt. I suspect that his real influence is yet to come, and will be exercised upon those Canadian historians who settle down to study the Canada of 1867 to 1914, who fall under the spell of the Bystander and come to see how shrewd were his comments upon current events, how enlightening his criticism of the nature of Canadian nationality, and how far-reaching his conception of the place of Canada in the English-speaking world.

Goldwin Smith was born in 1823, the son of a well-to-do physician in Reading. He received the typical training of the English scholar and gentleman of his day. He was sent to Eton in 1836, went up to Oxford in 1841, and won his BA in 1845. A brilliant classical student, he became on graduation a candidate for a fellowship at Queen's. But already he was marked out as a coming man in the little group of reformers in the university, and he was defeated for the fellowship by an obscure rival who was supported by the ecclesiastical party in the college.

This was the beginning for him of a struggle in which he was to play a part for the next twenty years in the university. Oxford was then almost entirely under clerical control, and it was only beginning to awake from the long intellectual torpor of the eighteenth century. Academical duty, Goldwin Smith tells us in his *Reminiscences*, was lost in the theological fray. The great question in his student days was, of course, the controversy over Newman. Looking back on it in his old age he declared that "the confluence of Newmanism with Romanism seems as natural as the confluence of two drops of water on a window-pane, and perhaps fraught with consequences little more momentous to humanity." But in the 1840s and 1850s he threw himself vigorously into the efforts of the little group of liberal reformers who were fighting against both Newman and his opponents, who were striving to emancipate Oxford altogether from its ecclesiastical atmosphere and its clerical control, and as he put it himself, to restore it to the nation. After the failure at Queen's he won a fellowship at University College. In 1850 he was appointed assistant-secretary of the Royal Commission of Inquiry which the reformers succeeded in having set up;

and he served also as secretary of the later Parliamentary Commission which drafted the legislation of 1854 and so made the first breach in ecclesiastical monopoly. The long and bitter struggle against the ecclesiastical party in the university coloured all his later thinking. He became a zealot for the removal of privileges and especially of religious privileges; he preached the separation of Church and State, and he continued to be a passionate anticlerical all his life.

His connection with the Royal and Parliamentary commissions introduced him to London society and to public life there. For some time he read law. In 1855 he became a member of the staff of the newly founded *Saturday Review* and began to distinguish himself as a political and literary controversialist. An admirer of Peel, he went with the Peelites to the liberal side of politics after the great disruption over the Corn Laws. In 1858, while still a young man of thirty-five years, he was appointed Regius Professor of Modern History at Oxford; and he returned to active work in the university, already a marked man on the liberal side both in the internal academic politics of Oxford itself and in the wider field of national affairs.

How Goldwin Smith conceived his function of professor of history is somewhat difficult to judge. His inaugural lecture in 1859 presents the honours History school as a discipline in preparing young men of the upper classes for public life. That it should be also a discipline for the training of scholars, of historians, does not seem to have been part of his ambition. He himself never settled down to research, and he has left behind him no great work which recreates and reinterprets for us a past period of history. Sometimes one is bound to wonder whether he would not have been a happier man had he devoted his life to his favourite period of early seventeenth-century Puritan England and anticipated the work of those later heroes of research, successors of his in the Oxford chair, Professors Gardiner and Firth.

In 1861 the American Civil War broke out. It is evident now that the Civil War was the turning point in Goldwin Smith's life. As a leader among the Liberals at Oxford he was already tending

apparently to become more and more immersed in current controversies; perhaps he was finding the ecclesiastical and conservative tone of the university more and more uncongenial and was
beginning to long for a wider sphere of activity. The American
struggle produced a sharp cleavage of opinion in England. "Society" in general, the governing classes and the Church, violently
espoused the cause of the South; and their chief journalistic organ,
the London *Times*, set itself to stir up ill-will between England and
the North. On the other side stood Cobden and Bright and the
Manchester Liberals, a few prominent intellectuals like John
Stuart Mill, and the industrial masses of northern England.
Goldwin Smith, with a small group of Oxford, Cambridge, and
London dons, joined the Manchester men. But they were a very
small minority in the society among which they moved.

Smith, who perhaps had a congenital tendency for finding
himself on the minority side, was stirred as he had never been
before. He became a pamphleteer. He began to deliver lectures
before great public audiences in London and in the North. This
activity brought him into personal contact with Cobden and Bright
and the other members of the Manchester School, and he quickly
found in their midst, rather than at Oxford, his spiritual home. In
1864 he went out to visit America, more or less as an official
delegate from those sections of the English public who had taken
the side of the North. The Regius Professor of Oxford, bearing a
message of goodwill from the English democracy to the Northern
democracy of the United States, was fêted and received with
honour wherever he went in the States. He came back to England
confirmed in his belief that in America was the hope of the
English-speaking race. The tremendous popular success of his
American visit and the revelation of the intensity of anti-American
and anti-democratic feeling among the English governing classes
caused him to look more and more longingly across the Atlantic.

The direction in which his mind was moving during these Civil
War years is shown in his private letters. Thus in 1864, before his
American visit, he writes to Charles Eliot Norton: "For my own
part I have fairly thought my way out of social and political

Feudalism and out of the State Church which is its religious
complement; and my intellect and heart are entirely with those who
are endeavouring to found a great community on the sounder as
well as the happier basis of social justice and free religious convic-
tions.'' He gives a fuller revelation of his mind in a speech which
he delivered at Boston in the course of his tour. It shows a Goldwin
Smith to which later Canadians are hardly accustomed, not the
sarcastic and destructive critic but the preacher expounding his
faith in a mood of the highest exaltation.

"To America, though an alien by birth, I am, as an English
Liberal, no alien in heart. . . . England bore you, and bore you not
without a mother's pangs. For the real hour of your birth was the
English Revolution of the seventeenth century, at once the saddest
and the noblest period of English history. . . . In England the
Revolution of the seventeenth century failed. It failed, at least, as
an attempt to establish social equality and liberty of conscience.
The feudal past, with a feudal Europe to support it, sat too heavy
on us to be cast off. . . . The nation had gone a little way out of the
feudal and hierarchical Egypt; but the horrors of the unknown
wilderness and the memory of the fleshpots overpowered the hope
of the Promised Land; and the people returned to the rule of
Pharaoh and his priests amid the bonfires of the Restoration. . . .
But the yoke which in the mother country we had not the strength
to throw off, in the colony we escaped; and here, beyond the reach
of the Restoration, Milton's vision proved true, and a free community was founded. . . . Yet in England the party of Cromwell and
Milton still lives. It still lives; and in this great crisis of your
fortunes, its heart turns to you. On your success ours depends.
Now as in the seventeenth century the thread of our fate is twined
with the thread of yours. An English Liberal comes here, not only
to watch the unfolding of your destiny, but to read his own. . . .
The soldiers of the Union are not Puritans, neither are the planters
Cavaliers. But the present civil war is a vast episode in the same
irrepressible conflict between Aristocracy and Democracy. . . .
The England of Charles and Laud has been against you; the
England of Hampden, Milton and Cromwell is on your side.''

While his mind was full of conceptions such as these, there occurred an event in his personal life which was decisive for his future. In 1866 his father, who had long retired from practice and was living as a country gentleman near Reading, suffered an injury in a railway accident, which produced a mental derangement. Goldwin Smith, a devoted son, was the only member of the family free and able to look after him. He threw up his professorship at Oxford and for two years was in almost daily attendance upon his father. Then he was compelled to leave home for a couple of days to attend to some business. While he was away his father committed suicide. The shock prostrated the son, and it was a long time before he fully recovered from it. The tragedy made all his old associations in England seem unbearable. Just at this time he met Andrew White, who invited him to join his staff in the newly created Cornell University. Smith accepted the invitation and came to America in 1868.

Life in the little rural village in northern New York confirmed him in his belief in the essential soundness of the American democratic experiment; and he was often accustomed in later years to contrast his own experience of the American people with that of the hypercritical English visitors who saw only the unlovely side of American democracy in the big cities. But apparently he found the task of teaching the very immature students of Cornell not altogether congenial. At any rate in 1871 he moved north to Toronto and settled here amongst relatives, continuing to go back periodically to Cornell to give courses of lectures. In 1875 he married Mrs. Boulton, the mistress of the Grange, and became a Torontonian for the rest of his life.

Several times during his early years on this side of the ocean he was invited back to England to enter politics on the Liberal side, and was offered safe constituencies in the North. He was invited to come back to Oxford as Master of University College. Later on, when the Home Rule struggle was at its height in the 1880s, the Unionist Liberals invited him to come back and lend his voice in Parliament against the dismemberment of the United Kingdom, a cause about which he became almost as passionate as he had been in his preaching against the dismemberment of the American

Union. But he resisted all temptations and remained in Canada. He must often, when being bitterly reviled in Toronto for his political views, have looked back with some regret to the career that a man with his intellectual abilities might have had in Oxford and in England. He was keenly conscious of the narrow stage upon which Canadian actors must play their part and of the limited audience before whom they perform. He was to learn to his sorrow that the influence which an intellectual can exercise in Canadian public affairs is severely limited. For in Canada there is little of that personal intercourse between practical statesmen and university dons which is a unique and charming feature of English life, raising the intellectual level of politics and saving the universities from becoming the breeding ground of PH Ds.

Before he left England Goldwin Smith had published another work, which, on the whole, seems to me to be the finest thing he ever wrote and which has been rather undeservedly forgotten. The Trent incident at the end of 1861, with its threat of war between England and the Northern States, raised the question of how Canada should be defended. In the spring of 1862 the Canadian legislature unceremoniously threw out a Militia Bill which had been drafted under the advice of Imperial staff officers; and the sequel was a long and acrimonious controversy between colony and mother country, which was carried on both in official despatches and in newspaper editorials. The defence crisis, coming on top of Canada's protective tariff of 1859, accentuated the tendency in England to discuss separation as the ultimate goal to which the colonies were inevitably drifting. Goldwin Smith entered the discussion with a series of letters to the chief liberal London paper, *The Daily News*. He gathered the letters together in a book entitled *The Empire*, which he published in 1863. They form the most perfect embodiment that we have of the imperial, or rather anti-imperial, doctrines of the Manchester school. They are written in what is for him a buoyant and high-spirited tone; for the writer believed that he was expressing the opinions of the most intelligent Englishmen whose minds were not biased by special interest.

The Empire is full of the usual Manchester arguments about the extravagance of maintaining colonies who close their markets to the products of the mother country and make no contribution to imperial defence. But it is more interesting to us today for the leading idea which runs through the book, the conception of Canada as potentially a new nation in a New World. "England," he writes, "has long promised herself the honour of becoming the mother of free nations. Is it not time that the promise should be fulfilled? . . . We are keeping the Colonies in a perpetual state of political infancy, and preventing the gristle of their frames from being matured and hardened into bone. . . . We have given them all that we really have to give — our national character, our commercial energy, our aptitude for law and government, our language. We have given them the essence of our constitution — free legislation, self-taxation, ministerial responsibility, personal liberty, trial by jury. The accidents of that constitution—the relics of the feudal world in which it was wrought—we can no more give them than we can give them our history or our skies. England is a European aristocracy, Canada is an American democracy. . . . I am no more against Colonies than I am against the solar system. I am against dependencies, when nations are fit to be independent. . . . But grant that Canada cannot stand as a nation by herself, it is with a nation in America, not with a nation in Europe, that she must ultimately blend. . . . And while she remains a province, Canada is, in fact, insensibly blending with the United States. . . . As a province she cannot form the independent character or assume the clear lineaments of a nation. . . . There is but one way to make Canada impregnable, and that is to fence her round with the majesty of an independent nation."

Was it not a cruel joke of fate that the man who dreamed this splendid vision of an independent Canadian nation should have been destined to live thirty-nine years in Toronto, the home of the United Empire Loyalists and the Loyal Orange Lodges?

But while he called upon Canada to undertake the responsibility of nationhood, Goldwin Smith did not mean that colonial nationality should involve the complete breaking of the tie with the mother country. "What is proposed is, not that Canada shall cease to be a Colony of England, but that she shall cease to be a dependency. . . . Is there any reason why, after the separation of the Governments, natives of Canada should not still be allowed, on coming to reside within the pale of English law, to become British citizens, to acquire all kinds of property, and to exercise, if otherwise duly qualified, all political rights? Is there any reason why Canada should not keep the old flag, with such difference as the Heralds' College may require? . . . These cravings for a grand unity are destined to find their fulfilment in the moral and intellectual, rather than in the political sphere.''

The truth is that the new British Commonwealth of Nations which we have been working out since 1914 bears a remarkable resemblancc to the ideas of the Manchester men in the 1860s. They saw far more clearly than their successors, the Imperialists of the 1880s and 1890s, the one essential fact, the fact of colonial nationality; and they welcomed it gladly. They did not believe that the young colonial nations could indefinitely remain within the political orbit of Great Britain. They did not believe that colonial nationality was compatible with the political centralization of the empire. We have retained more of the political and legal ties than they thought possible, especially the tie of the Crown. But most of these are now the harmless playthings of constitutional lawyers. The despised Manchester men have turned out to be much better prophets of the future course of imperial development than either Disraeli or Chamberlain.

Though he preached the gospel of Canadian nationality as against a colonial dependence upon England, it is clear from several passages in *The Empire* and in other writings that already before he left England Smith was impressed with the idea that the natural destiny of Canada was absorption in the United States. But he arrived in Canada in 1871 just when the country (or rather perhaps that part of it which centred about Toronto and Montreal) was in the first flush of national enthusiasm after the achievement of Confederation. Several leading public men, among them Alexander Galt on the Conservative side and L. S. Huntingdon on the Liberal side, were talking openly about independence. There was a feeling in the air, which was quickly sensed by the Oxford professor still alert for the potentialities of the New World, that great deeds were about to be performed, that all things were possible now that Canadian public men had shown their capacity to rise out of the muck of party politics and to join hands in creating "a new nationality".

The first result of this national impulse in the literary field was the launching, in January, 1872, of *The Canadian Monthly and National Review*. "It is hoped," said the publishers, "that the effort to give an organ, in the form of a periodical, to the intellectual life of Canada, is now made under better auspices than before. There has been of late a general awakening of national life, which has probably extended to the literary and scientific sphere, and special circumstances have favoured the publishers in obtaining literary assistance in the conduct of their Magazine." The special circumstances consisted in the arrival of Goldwin Smith in Toronto. He joined heartily in the new venture. In the second number of the *Canadian Monthly* appears the first article under the pen name which was to become so famous in Canada — "A Bystander". Very soon he was contributing a regular feature in the journal, a monthly commentary on current affairs, which he kept up, along with other contributors, till the end of 1874. He assisted in other ways also. We find him writing to Professor Max Müller of Oxford, asking him to procure some German stories which could be published in translation in the new magazine. "They hope," he writes in explaining the new venture to his friend, "to stop the process which is at present going on of intellectual annexation to the United States."

More important than this activity was another with which Goldwin Smith soon became connected. In Toronto a group of young romantics launched the "Canada First" movement, and sought the counsel and guidance of the Oxford professor who had so distinguished himself in England by his advocacy of Canadian nationality. The young men of "Canada First" were never quite sure whether their watchword meant political independence or not, and whether their function was to liberalize the Liberal party, or to found a new third party, or merely to help in creating a deeper consciousness of the implications of the new nationality among the community at large. But in 1874 they founded the National Club in Toronto, and Goldwin Smith became its first president. Edward Blake seemed to be their obvious political leader, and his great Aurora speech of 1874, with its declaration that we are "four millions of Britons who are not free", was taken up by them with enthusiasm. What they welcomed especially was Blake's tendency to discuss the broader issues of Canadian affairs and to emancipate himself from mere party warfare.

In April, 1874, appeared the first number of a new weekly journal in Toronto, *The Nation*, started as the organ of "Canada First" to preach the new nationalism. In January, 1875, Goldwin Smith dropped his connection with the *Canadian Monthly*, which now seemed fairly launched, and joined the *Nation*, becoming one of its chief editorial writers. But already the "Canada First" movement had been causing alarm in the minds of the regular party leaders and journals; and the *Globe* and the *Mail*, the two party dailies in Toronto, united to crush it. The *Globe* was especially ferocious in its attacks because it feared that Blake, if he listened to the blandishments of "Canada First", might lead off a large section of the Reformers in a break from the Brown-Mackenzie fold. A convenient method of intimidating Blake was to attack the Oxford professor; and upon Goldwin Smith through 1874 and 1875 it poured out its wrath. He was accused, when he discussed independence as the manifest destiny of Canada, of furthering a cause which meant simply revolution, of advocating a policy which would put in jeopardy the material, social, and religious interests of every individual in the Dominion; and his accuser announced that he was worthy of "a traitor's trial and a traitor's doom". Smith and his friends replied vigorously in the *Nation*, claiming the right to free discussion, denouncing the attempt to crush political independence by personal slander, and vaunting their determination to rescue Toronto from the journalistic despotism of George Brown. In the spring of 1875 the Blake section of the Reformers started a daily paper, *The Liberal*, in opposition

128   FRANK UNDERHILL

to the *Globe* in Toronto, and Smith lent his pen occasionally to this
journal also. But the *Globe*, or some other influence, was effective. The *Liberal* petered out after a few months. Blake returned to
party orthodoxy and became a member of the Mackenzie cabinet.
And the "Canada First" movement gradually disintegrated. The
Nation, its organ, eased publication in the fall of 1876.

Goldwin Smith was discouraged and disgusted. He was never
afterwards quite able to forgive Blake for what seemed to him, as
he looked back, the desertion under fire of the one political
movement in Canada that showed promise of raising the intellectual and moral level of Canadian public life, and of turning the
country's attention to something more significant than the ignoble
struggle of party machines for the spoils of office. Smith, as all his
life showed, was easily discouraged and disgusted. After the
failure of "Canada First" he reached the conclusion, which was
fortified by all his later experience, that the Canadian people
simply hadn't in them the capacity for making a nation.

Nevertheless, he still looked forward to playing an active part in
the community of which he was now a citizen. In the middle of the
1870s he was thinking seriously of seeking a seat in the Ontario
Legislature so that he could get into closer touch with the real daily
life of the ordinary Canadian. Sir John Macdonald, with whom, in
spite of the Pacific Scandal, he was on terms of friendly intimacy
through the 1870s, encouraged him in this idea and held out hopes
that he might become Minister of Education when the Conserva-
tives succeeded, as John A. Macdonald was sure they were just on
the point of doing, in ousting Oliver Mowat from office. In 1878
Smith supported Macdonald in the campaign for the National
Policy, and spoke at one of the campaign meetings. It is significant
that he welcomed the National Policy, though he was a good
disciple of Adam Smith and Richard Cobden, because it was a
declaration of national tariff autonomy in opposition to the tendency, of which he thought Brown and Mackenzie were guilty, to
curry favour with British industrialists and the British Government.

In the meantime he was still active in journalism. Apparently he
ceased to write for the *Nation* early in 1876, several months before

it gave up the ghost. But in April, 1876, he was helping John Ross Robertson to start the *Evening Telegram*. "The *Telegram*," its editor announced to his readers, "is a newspaper. It has no political axes to grind. In the bickerings and animosities of factions it takes no part. In the schemes and plots of politicians it has no share." To the *Telegram* in its early months the Bystander contributed frequent long letters which were really special articles on various subjects of Canadian public interest. Goldwin Smith and Sir Alexander Galt were the *Telegram*'s two chief heroes in those days because of their independent stand in politics. Volume One, Number Fourteen, of the paper devotes almost one page (five solid columns) to reproducing an article of Goldwin Smith — on "The Immortality of the Soul". In September, 1876, the Bystander was writing letters to the editor entitled "Is Protection the Real Remedy?" and arguing for closer trade relations with the United States.

There is an interesting letter from Goldwin Smith in the *Telegram* of October 2, 1876, on the occasion of the demise of the *Nation*, in which he gives his somewhat gloomy conclusions about native Canadian periodicals. He points out what he was to repeat very often later on, that Quebec severs Ontario from the Maritimes not only in a political but also in a literary sense, and that the only market to which a high-class Canadian journal can look is Ontario and the English district about Montreal. The *Nation* had failed because it could not command a large enough market to meet the competition of English journals, and, what was far more formidable, of the periodical literature of the United States, under the most spirited and skilful management in the world. "Nothing can sustain the Canadian publishers against such competition except the prevalence of a patriotic feeling, of pride and interest in native productions; and if such a feeling exists neither I nor the publishers with whom I have been connected have been able to discern it."

Nevertheless, he continued to the end of his life in his stubborn effort to foster high-class independent journalism in Canada. In 1880 he began his own little personal magazine, *The Bystander*, with its motto "Not party but the people", in which perhaps is to be found his best Canadian writing. The *Bystander* ran as a monthly through 1880 and the first half of 1881, was dropped then, while he went on a visit home to England, and was revived as a quarterly for the year 1883. On December 6, 1883, appeared the first number of *The Week*, "an independent journal of Literature, Politics and Criticism", edited at the beginning by Charles G. D. Roberts. Goldwin Smith was part owner of the *Week* and he ceased publication of his *Bystander* at the end of 1883 to take up under the same pen name a weekly feature of the new journal, two or three columns on *Current Affairs*. Like its most distinguished contributor the *Week* stood in favour of Canadian independence and was highly critical of both Canadian political parties, though not as despondent about party government in general as was the *Bystander*.

Later in the 1880s the *Week* came under new control and turned against Goldwin Smith's ideas about the political destiny of Canada. So in 1889, when the campaign for better trade relations with United States was at its height, he revived his *Bystander* to fill what he thought a dangerous gap in the advocacy of Commercial Union, and twelve numbers of a new series of the *Bystander* appeared from October, 1889, to September, 1890.

But this was not the end of his journalistic efforts. In 1896, now an old man of seventy-three, he was induced by a group of young radical friends to join in yet another venture. *The Weekly Sun*, the organ of the Patrons of Industry, was in financial difficulties owing to the disintegration of patronism amongst the Ontario farmers. Goldwin Smith already had a connection with Ontario farm movements through his part in the Commercial Union campaign which had been much more popular among the farmers than among the protected industries of Toronto and other urban centres. He bought a controlling interest in the *Sun* and the familiar pen name of the Bystander appeared once more. From 1896 he continued to write from one to three columns regularly for the front page of the *Weekly Sun*, until his wife's death at the end of 1909 and his own accident early in 1910 made further writing impossible.

What effect did all this journalistic writing have upon Canadian intellectual life? We must remember that at the same time Goldwin

Smith was writing books of one kind or another, his *Cowper* and his *Jane Austen* in the English Men of Letters series, his *Canada and the Canadian Question*, his *Essays on Questions of the Day*, his *Irish History and the Irish Question*, his political histories of the United States and of Great Britain, various booklets on religious questions, not to mention a host of articles in English journals like the *Fortnightly* and the *Nineteenth Century*, letters to the London *Times* and the New York *Sun*, letters and book reviews in Godkin's New York *Nation*; and a good part of this material must also have reached many of his Canadian audience.

No one today can read for long in Canadian journalism from the 1870s to the early 1900s without realizing how much higher a standard of writing the Bystander provided than most of his Canadian contemporaries. His comments on current affairs have behind them a rich store of historical knowledge upon which the writer constantly draws, and they show a range of interest which was lamentably lacking then, as it is lacking today, in Canadian journalism. He took his readers not only into Canadian politics but into American and British and continental European affairs as well. He could discuss Gladstone and Salisbury familiarly as men whom he had known as equals, and could deal with men like Morley, Chamberlain, Rosebery, Asquith, and Balfour as mere juniors. He lived to write obituary notices of all the great Victorians, and some of these magisterial criticisms, perhaps more than anything else in his writings, make one feel what a difference there was between the imported standards of London and Oxford and the native standards of Toronto. But the outstanding feature of his political writing is that he saw contemporary politics as only part of a world-wide intellectual movement. The breakdown of the old religious beliefs, the rise of science, the movement of feminism ("the sexual revolution", as he used to call it), the onward sweep of new socialistic movements in Europe, the slow drift of his own peaceful Victorian civilization into the madness of a world war, all these deeper undercurrents of human affairs drew his interest; and over against them he set the dismal pettiness of our parochial Canadian politics. To a modern reader the Bystander's writing shines out amidst the Canadian journalism of his day in somewhat the same way as Burke's speeches shine out amidst the windy oratory of the late eighteenth century in England. Let us put down at least this to his credit, that he paid his Ontario audience the compliment of believing that they were capable of appreciating the highest English culture.

About the style of his writing, as distinct from the matter of it, one need not say much. "Style," he said once, when asked how he achieved the austere simplicity and clarity which is the mark of his prose, "Style! I have no style, I merely wait for the mud to settle." There is not much Canadian journalistic writing which shows any sign of its author's having waited for the mud to settle.

But, of course, what Goldwin Smith is best remembered for in Canada is the body of doctrine as to Canada's destiny which he preached month in and month out. There are three or four main ideas around which all his journalistic writing is built. One is that of Canadian independence from Britain, to which reference has already been made. After 1870 this Manchester doctrine was gradually replaced in England by the movements for Imperial Federation and an Imperial Zollverein. Smith would have nothing to do with either movement. Again and again he called upon the Federationists to produce a concrete scheme so that it would be possible to discuss it. Again and again he pointed out that there was no hope of Canada's being induced to give up her control of trade to any imperial body and that she showed no signs of being willing to undertake the greater defence obligations which closer imperial union would involve. Especially did he object to the anti-American tendencies of these projects. "There is a federation which is feasible, and, to those who do not measure grandeur by physical force or extension, at least as grand as that of which the Imperialist dreams. It is the moral federation of the whole English-speaking race throughout the world, including all those millions of men speaking the English language in the United States, and parted from the rest only a century ago by a wretched quarrel."

In a closer imperial union, then, he saw no future. Every year he became more convinced that the real destiny of Canada lay rather in a closer union, commercial and political, with her neighbour upon this continent. The failure of "Canada First", the continuing cleavage between French and English, the geographical sectionalism of the country, all combined to make him pessimistic about the possibility of our achieving a separate nationality of our own upon this continent. Curiously enough, the development which made this a fixed idea in his mind was the building of the CPR, an exploit to which we look back now as the most magnificent expression in our history of our national faith in ourselves. Goldwin Smith, on the contrary, believed that the taking into Confederation of the great distant stretches of western prairie and of the still more distant province of British Columbia had produced a geographical structure in which no real unity was possible, and that the attempt to bind these vast territories together by the CPR would bankrupt the country, and was only an over-ambitious scheme of imperialist knights to carry out the project of attaching Canada to the Old World and making out of her an anti-American, anti-democratic Empire.

And this inescapable sectional and racial division of the country had its effect, as he was forever pointing out, in the party politics which developed after 1867. Macdonald kept things going by an unscrupulous policy of corruption, bribing first one section and then another, with special grants and public works. Unfortunately, such a policy was the only one possible in a country whose sections had so little in common. In his *Canada and the Canadian Question* Goldwin Smith quotes with relish the reply of a citizen of British Columbia of whom he had inquired what his politics were, and who answered promptly "Government Appropriations". "Not Cavour or Bismarck," he writes of Macdonald in another place, "is more fitted for his special task than he [Macdonald]. He has always had to deal with what have happily been called sinister interests. When he is gone, who will take his place? What shepherd is there who knows his sheep or whose voice the sheep know? Who else could make Orangemen vote for Papists and induce half the members for Ontario to help in levying on their province the necessary blackmail for Quebec? Yet this is the work which will have to be done if a general breakup is to be averted. When the shears of fate cut the thread of Sir John Macdonald's life what bond of union will be left?'' Briefly, of course, the answer to this pessimistic analysis of the means by which Canadian unity was maintained was that when Macdonald disappeared the Providence which watched over the destinies of the Canadian people could be trusted to produce a Laurier who was equally adept in the politics of ''Government Appropriations''.

So he stood for Continental Union because geographical sectionalism and racial and religious divisions made the smaller national union of Canada impracticable. Always, be it remembered, he repudiated the word ''Annexation'' with its suggestion of compulsion. The union he wished was one which would be freely and voluntarily entered into by both parties, like the Union of Scotland and England, and one to which he believed the mother country would give her blessing. That the disruption of the existing union with Great Britain would mean a breaking of old associations and a destruction of the continuity of our national life such as Canadians were not willing to contemplate he never grasped. ''I look forward,'' said Principal Grant of Queen's, ''to the happy reunion of our race with as much longing as Dr. Goldwin Smith, but to begin it with a second disruption is out of the question.'' That was the point which Goldwin Smith could not appreciate.

The controversy with Principal Grant, the last of many such controversies on this subject, took place in 1896, in the pages of the *Canadian Magazine*. By this time Goldwin Smith was an old man and had become more and more melancholy. He saw his own native country drifting, as it seemed to him, into the lowest type of demagoguery under Gladstone and then under Chamberlain, and the English democracy of which he had once had high hopes turning to confiscatory socialism. He called in vain for a Peel to appear and rally all the moderate elements of the community about him. At the same time the United States drifted into bimetallism and Bryanism. ''The American Commonwealth,'' he told his farmer readers in the *Weekly Sun* in 1896, ''is the greatest experiment ever made in popular government. The fate of popular government in all countries, notably in our own, must be largely decided by its result. . . . Bimetallism, even repudiation, is not the greatest factor in this crisis. All the elements of distress, disaffection, revolution and anarchy have for the first time banded themselves together against the life of a Commonwealth which is founded on property and the vital principle of which is liberty under the law.'' But when the republic escaped the peril of Bryanism it was only to plunge into a greater evil, the imperialistic adventure of the Spanish American War. ''The American Republic was the hope of democracy. . . . It promised to do something more than the Old World towards correcting the injustice of nature, equalizing the human lot, and making the community a community indeed. . . . Shall the American Republic follow its own destiny and do what it can to fulfil the special hopes which humanity has founded in it, or shall it slide into an imitation of European Imperialism?'' At the same time Britain became entangled in the Boer War; and, to his infinite disgust, Laurier allowed Canada to be entangled also. The two great branches of the Anglo-Saxon race, to whose ultimate reunion he had dedicated his life, seemed to be uniting only in a career of unscrupulous imperialism.

And when the Boer and the Spanish-American wars were over, there began to loom up the prospect of a still more terrible war between Britain and Germany. The last contributions of the Bystander to the *Weekly Sun* were mainly taken up with warning Canada not to let herself again be involved in the adventures of British Imperialism. ''What a close to the Peelonian era!'' he wrote to an old English friend in 1900, ''I well remember the Reform Bill of 1832 with its golden hopes of a reign of reason and peace.'' The sun of humanity was behind a cloud, and perhaps the Bystander was not altogether sorry to leave the world before his worst fears as to the future could be realized.

The problem of our Canadian nationality, of the conditions which have determined its development in the past, of the possibilities which lie before it in the future, is the fundamental question that confronts any student of Canadian affairs. It is because Goldwin Smith's mind was exercised about this problem for so long a time and because he brought to it such a store of experience and philosophy from an older civilization that he is so much worth studying. Why has the growth of nationality been so slow and uncertain? In the first number of the *Canadian Monthly* of 1872 there is a long editorial discussing why British America had up to then produced no literature worth speaking of and pointing out that it was still a pioneer community from which the finer fruits of civilization could not yet be expected. We are still making the same defence of ourselves in 1933. For our political history shows the same perplexing lack of growth as our cultural history. The gristle of our frame has never matured and hardened into bone. As Sir John Willison remarked cynically at the close of his life, with every change of government in Canada we are made into a nation over again. And the student of Canadian history, as he puzzles over these conditions, gets an overpowering feeling that he is going round and round inside a squirrel cage. He begins to wonder whether Goldwin Smith's interpretation of events was quite so wide of the mark after all. I expect that when the definitive history of the Dominion is at last written it will contain long and frequent quotations from the Bystander.

He died in 1910. I was an undergraduate in the University of Toronto at that time, and I can still remember well the day of his funeral. It was in June at the time of Convocation. The City of Toronto, which had long repudiated with loathing most of the opinions of its most distinguished citizen, decided to give him a public funeral; and the service was held in Convocation Hall at the university. Officials from various government bodies attended. The federal government sent its young Minister of Labour, the Hon. W. L. Mackenzie King. A few of us students were recruited to serve as ushers. But the day of the funeral dawned cold, windy, and rainy. Gusts of rain swept across the university lawn as the funeral cortege arrived and as it left. And we ushers were hardly needed, because so few of the public attended. I have always thought that that gloomy funeral day symbolized most fittingly the relations of Goldwin Smith with his fellow-citizens of Canada. They remained aloof from each other and estranged to the end.

What are we to say now, today, about Goldwin Smith's opinions? Canada has become an independent nation, as he originally wished. But we have achieved our independence without the breach in the British connection that he thought to be necessary. We have not united politically with the United States, as he later wished, though he was right in foreseeing that the lives of the two North American peoples would interpenetrate each other more and more closely every year. So closely, in fact, that many of our intellectuals today are deploring our dependence upon the United States just as he in his day deplored our dependence upon Britain. Like him, they seem to have lost faith in our Canadian capacity to live an individual, autonomous, self-respecting Canadian life of our own. We spent the century from the Rebellion of 1837 down to the outbreak of war in 1939 in achieving our independence of Great Britain. We are going to spend the next century, from the Ogdensburg and Hyde Park agreements of 1940 down to somewhere about 2040 in maintaining our independence of the United States. And, no doubt, the second century is going to be a tougher experience than the first.

But there is no need for us to wring our hands in despairing defeatism or to start on witch-hunts looking for the traitors who have led us into this dire peril. The trouble with Goldwin Smith, his root weakness, the reason for his loss of faith in his fellow Canadians, was that he lived too far aloof from them. As he grew old, he sat there in his library in the Grange, insulated by his bookshelves from the teeming life of Toronto all around him and from the life of Canada beyond Toronto. What he needed was to get out and meet a few ordinary Canadians and become intimate with them — not intellectuals from the university but just ordinary Canadians. And this is what our critical university intellectuals of today need to restore their faith in the capacity of Canada to survive as a Canadian community. Faith is something that comes from living and not from purely intellectual processes.

Sursum corda! Let us lift up our hearts. We have come a long distance since Goldwin Smith's day, and there is no need for us to sink once more into his despair. Obviously Canada is no longer just the four northerly extensions of the American fertile belt, which was all he could discern in 1891. Our statesmanship has proved anything but bankrupt. Now that we are trying ourselves out on the stage of world power politics, we can afford to be proud of the skill with which our spokesmen are giving expression to a Canadian point of view and the wisdom with which they are looking after Canadian interests. *Sursum corda!*

But at the same time, as I hope I have shown, many of Goldwin Smith's criticisms have a remarkably up-to-date ring about them; and it will not do us any harm now and then to go back and restudy the picture of our weaknesses as he painted it at the end of the nineteenth century.

GEORGE GRANT

Philosophy in the Mass Society

WHEREAS animals live by instinct and therefore do what they do directly, we can decide between alternatives, and this choice is possible because we can reflect on how we are going to act. We can formulate general rules or principles which serve as guides among the innumerable possibilities open to us and which give some degree of consistency to our lives as a whole. Thus men who make the pursuit of wealth the chief activity of their lives have, at least to some degree, formulated the principle that all their actions will be as much as possible subordinated to that end. But also we know that how we do live is not always how we ought to live. It therefore becomes of supreme importance that we think deeply as to what are the right principles by which we should direct our lives. Through the ages the thinking about such principles has been called "moral philosophy". Morality is the whole sphere of actions to which we can apply the categories right and wrong. Moral philosophy is the attempt by reflection to make true judgements as to whether actions are right or wrong. The making of such judgements requires knowledge of the principles of right, and knowledge to apply those principles to our particular situation.

The process of thinking through our lives in this way is of course something that each person can only do for himself. As Luther once said, "A man must do his own believing as he must do his own dying." There is, however, value in discourse on the subject, particularly in considering what men have thought about these matters through the ages. Our minds are not separate, and we move towards the truth only as we are willing to learn from the full weight of what the thought of the past and the present have to tell us. Humanity has been called an inherited deposit, and we only become fully human as we make that deposit our own.

The historical situation of the West, and of Canadians in particular, calls for the frankest and most critical look at the principles of right in which we put our trust. The world situation has been described so often: the existence of two rival power blocs both with instruments of total destruction, and the living in an age when we have launched on the conquest of space aided by our new technological mastery. In political and pulpit rhetoric, we hear repeated over and over that our conquest of nature has taken us to the point where we can destroy the human race. This is, indeed, an obvious cliché, but still true.

Not only this world picture makes our situation new, but also the very texture of our North American society.[1] On this continent the modern mass age has arrived as to no other people in the world. North America is the only society that has no history of its own before the age of progress, and we have built here the society which incarnates more than any other the values and principles of the age of progress. Inevitably, other cultures are moving in the same direction. In 1957 it became obvious to the world how fast the Soviet Union was moving towards the scientific society. There, a people, scientifically backward forty years ago, have so concentrated their efforts, under the direction of a great philosophic faith, Marxism, that they have caught up with and in certain fields surpassed our society with its much deeper rational and scientific traditions. So far, however, modern scientific civilization has been most extensively realized in North America. Ours is the world of mass production and its techniques, of standardized consumption and standardized education, of wholesale entertainment and almost wholesale medicine. We are formed by this new environment at all the moments of our work and leisure — that is, in our total lives.

This world finds its chief creative centre in the Great Lakes region of North America, and spreads out from there as the dominant pattern of culture which shapes the rest of the continent. The Canadian heart of it is that vast metropolis which expands along the shores of Lake Ontario, with the old city of Toronto as its heart. It is the society of the continental chain stores and the automobile empires — the agents of which spread their culture through the rest of Canada. I, for instance, live in a little peninsula on the fringes of Canada which two generations ago had a rather simple but intelligible agricultural, commercial, and military culture of its own. Even in the ten short years I have lived in Halifax, I have watched with amazement the speed with which the corporation empires have taken over this old culture and made it their own. This culture of monolithic capitalism creates the very fabric of all our lives.

Two characteristics above all distinguish this culture from others that have existed. First, it is scientific; it concentrates on the domination of man over nature through knowledge and its application. This dominance of man over nature means that we can satisfy more human needs with less work than ever before in history. This characteristic of our society is generally recognized. What is less often recognized is that this society, like all others, is more than simply an expression of the relationship of man to nature; it also exemplifies a particular relationship of man to man; namely, some men's dominance over other men. All our institutions express the way in which one lot of men dedicated to certain ends impose their dominance over other men. Our society is above all the expression of the dominance that the large scale capitalist exerts over all other persons. And what makes our modern society something new in history is the new ways that these concentrated economic, political, and military élites have of imposing social dominance over the individual. The paradox indeed is this: so great is the power that society can exert against the individual that it even subjects to dominance those very élites who seem to rule. Thus at this stage of industrial civilization, rule becomes ever more impersonal, something outside the grip of any individual. We can say, then, that ours is the society of late state capitalism.

This new society and its intimate shaping of our lives presents to us in a particularly pressing way the need for moral philosophy. I do not mean by this anything so childish as that we can think simply about what in this culture we should accept and what reject. Individuals are not in a position where they can accept and reject their culture in this simple way and shape history by such choices alone. We cannot choose to be independent of the forces that make our mass culture far too profound simply to be thought away. The belief that the forms of society can be easily changed by our choices is a relic of the faith in liberalism, and as limited as most of that liberal faith. Philosophical faith is something rather different. Its hope is more indirect. As we live in these conditions of mass culture, we come to recognize them as profoundly new and this newness forces us to try to understand what they mean. We ask what it is that man has created in this new society. And as we try to see what we are, there arises an ultimate question about human nature and destiny. And such questions are what philosophy is. What I mean by philosophy arising out of such a situation is that so totally new is our situation in history that we are driven to try and redefine the meaning of human history itself—the meaning of our own lives and of all lives in general. The fixed points of meaning have so disappeared that we must seek to redefine what our fixed points of meaning are. From this reassessment the shaping of our society will ultimately proceed.

The most remarkable of modern philosophers, Hegel, expressed this by saying, "The owl of Minerva only takes its flight at twilight." What he means is that human beings only pursue philosophy, a rigorous and consistent attempt to think the meaning of existence, when an old system of meaning is coming to the end of its day. He does not imply in the remark any ultimate pessimism, for pessimism is by definition always vain. He does not imply that philosophy only arises when it is too late. Too late for what? What he means is that we take thought about the meaning of our lives when an old system of meaning has disappeared with an old society, and when we recognize that the new society which is coming to be raises new questions which cannot be understood within the old system.

It is certain that in Canada our old systems of meaning, which suited the world of a pioneering, agricultural society with small commercial centres, have disappeared with the world they suited. And the more that people live in the new mass society, the more they are aware that the old systems of meaning no longer hold them, and the less they are able to see any relation between the old faiths and the practical business of living. For instance, the firm old Protestantism, with its clear appeal to the Bible as the source of meaning, honestly and directly held the large part of English-speaking Canada a hundred years ago. It no longer does so. The mass of people no longer find in it that unambiguous meaning within which they can live their lives. This is truer than it was a generation ago; it is truer this year than it was last year. How many of the old-type, firm, and unequivocal Protestants can be found, outside certain rural areas and apart from the older generation?

Of the Roman Catholic tradition I know much less, nor do I know how much certainty its members find in its ancient wisdom. It has always been a minority tradition in North American society, outside French-speaking Canada. And I, for one, am certain that a people who have passed through Protestantism can never go back to a traditional Catholicism.[2]

I am not here concerned with the truth or falsity of Christianity or with the question of what loyalty men should grant to established religious organizations. To say that a particular system of meaning which arose from a particular form of Christianity no longer holds men's minds is not to identify Christianity with that particular form and therefore to brand it as inadequate. What Jesus Christ did is not ultimately dependent on its interpretations. What I am saying is simply that we cannot rest in old systems of meaning. Always in human history at periods of great change, when in that change the most sensitive feel the most deeply insecure, there has been the tendency to seek an answer to that insecurity by turning to the certainties of the past. Therapies which turn back the wheel of history are proposed as remedies for that insecurity. Such reactionary experiments are always vain. In a period when meaning has become obscure, or to use other language, when God seems absent, the search must be for a new authentic meaning which includes within itself the new conditions which make that search necessary. It must be a philosophical and theological search.

Yet, as soon as we have admitted the need for that search, we must admit that our very society exerts a terrible pressure to hold us from that search. Every instrument of mass culture is a pressure alienating the individual from himself as a free being. In late capitalism the individual finds more and more that responsibility for his own life lies not with himself but with the whole system. Work is after all a necessity for civilization and work is always organized in an economic apparatus. And our economic apparatus is increasing rationalized: work is more and more divided into specialized functions. In this situation the individual becomes (whether on the assembly line, in the office, or in the department store) an object to be administered by scientific efficiency experts. The human being is made to feel that he can best get along if he adjusts his attitudes to suit the collective institutions which dominate his life. Most of us know the power of these collective institutions and what they do to a person who will not conform to their demands.

This is not only true of our work but of our leisure. Modern culture, through the movies, newspapers, and television, through commercialized recreation and popular advertising, forces the individual into the service of the capitalist system around him. As has been said so often, in the popular television programmes the American entertainment industry reproduces the hackneyed scenes of family life as the source of amusement. The American family (though made more prosperous than the ordinary family so that the acquisitive desire will be aroused) is described and exalted in its life, which is so perfectly adjusted to the world of life insurance, teen-age dating, and the supermarket. This, of course, glorifies our society as it is. Here is the way all decent Americans live and here is the way all mankind should live. And this exaltation helps to entrap us in the very reality described, helps us to accept our world and its system. Entertainment is used to keep people happy by identifying life as it is with life as it ought to be. Art is used to enfold us in the acceptance of what we are, not as the instrument of a truth beyond us.

In the same way, religion is no longer an appeal to the transcendent and the infinite potentiality of the spirit. It is valued as something which holds society together and helps to adjust the individual to accept the organization as it is. The fact that a reliable member of society is seen as a church-goer becomes a motive for church attendance. Advertisements are put out: ''Take your children to church and make them good citizens.'' The ideal minister is the active democratic organizer who keeps the church running as a home of social cohesion and ''positive thinking''. Thus even the church is brought to serve the interests of the apparatus persuading the individual into conformity with its ends. All this, of course, makes it difficult for the individual in our society to see any point to that rational reassessment of life which I have called moral philosophy. The very system exerts pressure at every point against such an assessment.

What must be stressed in this connection is that reason itself is thought of simply as an instrument. It is to be used for the control of nature and the adjustment of the masses to what is required of them by the commercial society. This instrumentalist view of reason is itself one of the chief influences in making our society what it is; but, equally, our society increasingly forces on its members this view of reason. It is impossible to say which comes first, this idea of reason or the mass society. They are interdependent. Thought which does not serve the interests of the economic apparatus or some established group in society is sneered at as ''academic''. The old idea that ''the truth shall make you free'', that is, the view of reason as the way in which we discover the meaning of our lives and make that meaning our own, has almost entirely disappeared. In place of it we have substituted the idea of reason as a subjective tool, helping us in production, in the guidance of the masses, and in the maintenance of our power against rival empires. People educate themselves to get dominance over nature and over other men. Thus, scientific reason is what we mean by reason. This is why in the human field, reason comes ever more to be thought of as social science, particularly psychology in its practical sense. We study practical psychology in order to learn how other people's minds work so that we can control them, and this study of psychology comes less and less to serve its proper end, which is individual therapy.

This view of reason has found its most popular formulation in North America, in the philosophy known as pragmatism, famous in the writings of William James and John Dewey. This is not surprising, for it is in North America that control over nature and social adjustment has reached its most explicit development. Later on I wish to speak of pragmatism in detail as an important modern philosophy. At the moment I simply wish to emphasize that this philosophy, with its view of reason as an instrument, mirrors the actual life of our continent, in which individual freedom is subordinate to conformity.

Such an account of reason goes so deep into the modern consciousness that any other account is very difficult for a modern man to understand at all. Therefore, only by constant and relentless reflection on this modern idea can we hope to liberate ourselves from the naïve acceptance of it. Yet obviously the philosophic enterprise is only possible insofar as we have liberated ourselves from this view of reason.

Yet, as soon as one has considered the obstacles which society puts in the way of philosophic thought, one must assert the opposite, and express optimism about the possibility of philosophy in our society. Whatever else the industrial civilization may have done, it has eliminated the excuse of scarcity. Always before in history, the mass of men had to give most of their energy to sheer hard work because of the fact of scarcity. The conquest of nature by man through technology means human energy is liberated to attain objectives beyond those practically necessary. As this becomes ever more realized, vast numbers of men are able to devote their time to the free play of their individual faculties. The constraints once justified by the fact of scarcity can no longer in North America be justified on those grounds. Always before in history, if some few men were to be able to pursue the life of philosophy, it depended on the labour of others, who because of that labour were themselves removed from the possibility of the philosophic life. The ideal of human freedom the philosophers held up was always denied by their dependence upon the work of others. Such a contradiction becomes increasingly unnecessary. Reason, considered as domination over nature, has freed man from his enslavement to nature so that it is open to him to pursue the life of reason as more than simply domination. The world of mass production and consumption and the idea of social equality makes this possible. Whatever we may say against our society, we must never forget that.

Indeed, just as our industrial civilization creates the conditions of repression, it also creates the natural conditions of universal liberation: not only in the economic sense that people who are free from the necessity of hard work have the leisure to pursue ends beyond the practical, but also in the sense that an industrial society breaks down the old natural forms of human existence in which people traditionally found the meaning for their lives. In such a situation many persons are driven by the absence of these traditional forms to seek a meaning which will be their own.

Anybody who sees much of the young people of our big cities will know what I mean. They are freed from the pressing demands of scarcity at the same time as they are freed from the old framework of tradition. And this produces in them a state of high self-consciousness; they are immensely open to both good and evil. This does not mean simply that the end of scarcity makes possible a high level of self-consciousness to nearly all classes in society. A more subtle process is implied. However much the repressive elements of late industrial society may lie on us like chains, this very society is a fruit of the civilization of Europe: the civilization of rational theology, of the Reformation, and of the Enlightenment; a civilization which brought men a knowledge of themselves as free as had no other in the past. And these young people, whether they know it or not, hold in their very being the remnants of that tradition, the knowledge of themselves in their freedom, even if much else from that tradition has never been theirs. Thus knowing themselves as free, they know their freedom as standing against the pressures of the society which binds them in an impersonal grip. In such a society the best of them are open to the philosophic life with an intensity worthy of the greatest periods of human thought. How this happens is concretely expressed in the novels of J. D. Salinger. In the *New Yorker* of May, 1956, Salinger had a story called "Zooey", which describes just such people. One finds them among the youths wherever one goes in North America. God reigns and the salt cannot lose its savour.

What is sad about these young people is that our educational institutions cannot be ready to meet their needs. Our educational institutions at all levels are still largely formed by what is most banal in our society. They have lost what was best in the old European education. They are spiritually formed by the narrow practicality of techniques; they are immediately governed by ill-educated capitalists of narrow interest. But this very failure of our educational institutions is part of that alienation which will drive the best of our students to philosophy and theology. And these young people are the evidence that in our society profound philosophical thought is arising. They herald what may yet be, surprisingly, the dawn of the age of reason in North America.

DAVE GODFREY

Doomsday Idealism

*The Volunteer Back Inside the Great Castle of the Western World
Turns from the Televised Horrors of the Evening's War in Vietnam
and the Teletyped Spectacle of the Country's Cabinet Begging
Washington to Keep Our "Good Corporate Citizens" from De-
stroying Our Delicate Dollar and Confronts the Problems of the
World.*

RETURNING, there is only one clear, overwhelming thought:
gnat against elephant. Your work has been that of a gnat, clean-
faced and valiant, straining at the end of a tugrope against a
dysenteric, powerful, embittered, starving, self-tortured, awakening, ancient, immensely humane, knowing, and surprisingly un-
embittered elephant.

Abroad, there is always a multiplicity of response to these
immense problems of *le tiers monde*, of the new worlds, the
developing continents.

But once the volunteer has returned, there does seem to be at
least one similarity of reaction: a sense of quietude. Protests may
be written about the *Vancouver Sun*'s poor coverage of the Biafran
crisis, but not very hopefully. Canadian complacency (and ignorance) appears overwhelming. Volunteers on return tend to work
for CUSO, raising funds, giving speeches, aiding in selection.
There has been little rocking of the canoe; no large-scale protests
that Canada as a society is taking the wrong trail in her attitudes

and actions towards the new worlds.[1] This article is based on protest; this article will consider a CUSO TWO as a tool for Utopia-building, for I look upon Doom and Utopia as neighbours.

There are reasons for that quietude, of course, reasons beyond our massive and incredibly naive support of *Time* and the *Reader's Digest*. We all partake of, are part of, the myth of the Americas: Jack's as good as his master—as long as he works twice as hard—for self-interest maximizes profit: that myth wherein the individual solves his own problems and protects his own brood and pocket-book, while growing in stature and worldly rank through his "own" exertions.

And, more importantly, the immensity of these third-world problems stills the tongue.

For a type of paralysis sets in. The volunteer would seem the natural person to continue a Canada/*tiers monde* interaction. He can re-experience the problems specifically: in ragged cotton *boubous* see again one male cripple beggar leading one female blind beggar leading one male, armless beggar through the night streets of Dakar. He can also perceive them generally, in terms, let us say, of those overlaid maps (kwashiorkor prevalence, *per capita* income, famine expectancy, illiteracy per thousand, infant mortality, protein levels, doctors per thousand) which show, by their constant patternings, the way each abstracted problem ladles molten misery on the others.

But the volunteer is, must be, by the time of his return, conscious not only of these problems but of the incredible gulf between the energies at his command and the staggering, Kitimat-huge quantities that would be required for any genuine solution. Band-Aids are little help to the leper; by the time the Aswan Dam is completed (and by 1972 its waters and energy will help feed thirteen million people), thirteen million more Egyptians will inhabit that country.[2]

If he comes back from India, he knows that the valley of the Ganges River is one of the greatest stretches of flat alluvium in the world, often thousands of feet thick. Yet this vast expanse of class one and class two alluvial soil has been a focal point for famine during the past three years, despite two decades of modern technology freely applied towards India's food problem.[3]

To break the Malthusian stranglehold there, volunteerism is simply not enough. The key is applied energy. Energy that can produce food that can sustain man so that he can produce energy that can be directed towards the production of food. Yet, even at an Indian wage scale of thirteen cents per day, the human equivalent of one kilowatt-hour of electrical energy costs fifty cents.[4] That muscle power which can be fuelled from the land at this exorbitant rate cannot achieve one-tenth the agricultural production levels which are potentially there, if cheap energy for pumping water and fixing nitrogen were available.

Obviously, hundreds of Bobby Hulls and Whipper Billy Watsons willing to work at starvation wages would accomplish little; the energy would still be far too expensive. Slavery did not fade out because of man's nobility but simply because industry acknowledged that heat engines put it entirely out of the competitive picture. There is no rate of pay at which a Canadian pick-and-shovel labourer can live which is low enough to compete with the work of a steam shovel as an excavator.

If we require a clear and simple statistic, let us begin to examine this: a nuclear power station of about one-thousand-megawatts capacity installed in the Ganges Valley to power an NH_3 plant during eight months of the year, while driving irrigation pumps the other four months, could produce, on a small fraction of the Ganges land, 1.1 billion dollars' worth of wheat or an extra one hundred and fifty pounds of grain for each of the two hundred million people living in the valley.[5]

1.1 billion dollars' worth of wheat grown within the country; what volunteer thinks in those terms?

Such solutions are pragmatic rather than Utopian. The capital cost of one such complex (nuclear plant, power grid, wells, ammonia plant, etc.) would be 1.2 billion dollars or approximately the cost of ten days of our neighbour's little war in Vietnam. Then CUSO could say, I'm done. But is this what CUSO desires? Is this what CUSO or Canada or the castle nations of the North Atlantic are willing to provide? Or are even considering? What would it do to wheat markets if the world were well fed? What would it do to Massey-Ferguson if it became obvious that the new worlds should nuclear-base rather than petroleum-base their agriculture?

Back within the Canadian castle these questions keep intruding.

None of us would consider that we accept the world as a vast unchanging misery-laboratory, wherein those who are lucky enough to be aware of our world condition provide themselves with an unusual variety of experiential thrill by briefly learning and serving; let us call this the joy of leper-touching. Yet, if we are to deny that description, we must accept one of two alternatives: (a) that this misery and poverty will eventually encircle the globe and the wage scale in Victoria will fall to two hundred and eighteen dollars per annum, while kwashiorkor becomes prevalent in Ste. Anne de Beaupré — so that we inhabitants of the castle might as well learn what it means to suffer at once and under conditions of our own choosing, or (b) that, eventually, we and they are going to learn to ask the correct questions and perform the proper actions so that the entire world will enjoy our abundance and fertility.

Are we bold for one more Utopia? Even if it be of IGA and Wheat Board variety?

I know of no returned volunteer who even considers the possibility of kwashiorkor in Calgary. The other possibility, success, raises its own specific difficulties. At the moment, the rate of discovery of metal ores is slower than the human population increase; yet, the present cumulative total of metals — mined and refined by men through all history — is wholly employed in machines or structures, which, operating at limit capacity, can accommodate and benefit only forty-four per cent of living humanity.[6] Nor must we forget to ask; to what use have the castle people put their energy-inventions since 1900?

For the "I" which reached manhood within a CUSO experience is a particular one. Television may have been his third parent but the thought of doomsday was a constant companion. Aerial warfare was his birthmark and for him the sword which the tyrant Dionysius hung by a hair over the head of Damocles was a figure of speech which never needed explanation. Even as a child in Winnipeg (and what city could have been farther from Auschwitz), I watched the men of the realm play their world-game of black-out and air raid. We learned to read only to become aware of Hiroshima and the Nürnberg trials, of women and children tossed alive into quicklime; our adolescence taught us the non-heroic lessons of Korea and Hungary. Now. Returned? My own house is a way station for draft dodgers and military deserters; my children will be taught Judaism rather than the Christianity of the English and German and French empires; and my own students, the ones I prefer, can no longer quite, in the prewar way, deny all moral responsibility, but stand shivering and ineffectual, while the engineers jeer at their attempts to barricade the doors of the university to their own administration. An administration which, without fuss or self-questioning, sets up a committee to legalize and ratify Canada's position as a colony of the American economic empire by welcoming manufacturers of Vietnam armaments as *Personae non questae* into the university. The government says yes, says the university. We need the trade, says the government; after all, we have much of the bill for CUSO to pay and medicare to come.[7]

Reactions to such doomsday-heading and complicity-creating chains of events — events which encircle the individual's own petty burst of development — are relatively easy to predict. Few consider conquering the chain.

A quite large percentage are turning to that 1870 discovery of the American Indians, peyote, and to the synthetic psychedelics and to the idiosyncratic life,[8] attempting to prove by the particulars to their life habits that they do not belong to the species of man, if Auschwitz, Dresden, Hiroshima, Hungary, Korea, and Vietnam are to mark man's definitive characteristics.

The majority intensify the rituals of ordinary life, searching for a lost ceremoniousness with ever-increasing hecticness, seemingly content so long as the spirit of the Gross National Product appears well-fed and non-malevolent.[9]

A small percentage attempt what they can through the new social structures such as CUSO and the Company of Young Canadians. For them, perhaps, the sense of escape while abroad is similar to that of the hero in *Pilgrim's Progress* who remembered, only after all his beatings in Doubting Castle, that since entering he had carried the key that would release the bolt of any lock in Giant Despair's Castle.

But on return, the problems still seem immense and Canada far distant from them. The inevitable reaction to our long economic colonization of Quebec occupies front stage. Faced with a theoretical choice between the United States' definition of injustice as a failure to practise political libertarianism or the Soviet Union's definition of injustice as an attempt to practise political libertarianism without solving the economic dilemmas of poverty, the nation straddles the fence and hopes things won't get too worse before they get worse. We are a victim of the American paradox, for we admire their revolution-based democracy, where each man counts as one and none unequal, while we accept their right to exert hegemony over the hemisphere and increasingly over the world—a hegemony wherein obviously the Jack nation is far from as good as his master nation.[10] In such a context, it is pleasant to be reminded that in Vietnam there is a purpose to that massive investment of trillions of dollars which the castle nations have poured into aircraft energy-inventions since 1900:

Dixie Station [in the Vietnam Delta] had a reason. It was simple. A pilot going into combat for the first time is a bit like a swimmer about to dive into an icy lake. He likes to get his big toe wet and then wade around a little before leaping off the high board into the numbing depths. So it was fortunate that young pilots could get their first taste of combat under the direction of a forward air controller over a flat country in bright sunshine where nobody was shooting back with high-powered ack-ack. He learns how it feels to drop bombs on top of human beings and watch huts go up in a boil of orange flame when his aluminum napalm tanks tumble into them. He gets hardened to pressing the firing button and cutting people down like little cloth dummies, as they sprint frantically under him. He gets his sword bloodied for the rougher things to come.[11]

"I read the news today, oh boy." Where do we turn for answers?

If we are to consider a CUSO TWO, to examine the trowels and reactors of a new Utopia, we must face the dangers, look at the productive structures of our time, and search out the innovations of science and technology. The ecologists, the anthropologists, the liberal-activists, Mao, Nyerere, and the Joint Chiefs of Staff all have ideas or solutions. Which are useful? Necessary? Dangerous? How do we prevent the horror of Dixie Station and of Vietnam from being the pattern of our time?

Such aggressive behaviour against members of our own species has, of course, a far longer history than that of the castle nations themselves let alone their volunteers. The ecologists, notably K. Lorenz, have begun to investigate intra-specific aggressive behaviour not only in terms of its obvious benefits — balanced distribution of the species, selection of the strongest, and defence of the young — and its obvious great danger: the fixing within us hereditarily of hypertrophies of traits of killing and self-amassing of wealth; but in terms of the role aggression has played in the development of responsible, or communal, morality.[12] Lorenz finds the basis of morality not in Kantian reason, but in the necessary values which grew up within small warring tribal groups who directed their aggression outward and yet learned to control the same ability to kill when dealing with the members of their own warrior-group.

Rather than reason, he finds it is instinctive behaviour mechanisms which provide the dynamic source of friendship and love, warmth of feeling, appreciation of beauty, and the curiosity that strives toward scientific enlightenment. Our danger lies not in failing to defeat our "animal nature" but rather in denying causality, denying the effects of race history on our behaviour, in favour of an unproven, idealistic free will.

As Lorenz points out: in emphatic contrast to our knowledge of genes and atoms, we possess *no* immediate knowledge of the function or survival value of the majority of our established customs, notwithstanding our emotional conviction that they do in-

deed constitute high values. This applies just as equally to the
Soviet belief in economic equality as to the American belief in
political libertarianism and to the Canadian belief in patient compromise. Yet at the same time we are faced with an awesome
increase in our mechanical kill-power without any parallel development of cultural ritualizations which could act as inhibitors. The
invention of artificial weapons has totally upset the equilibrium of
killing-potential and social inhibitions. Forced to lay money on
one of two horses — a CUSO motivated by rational and idealistic
norms of human behaviour or a United States Air Force obviously
motivated by aggressive patterns of behaviour reaching back into
the Stone Age—a man would have to be an idiot to select the CUSO
horse.

The anthropologists, from whom we might expect a clearer description of our doomsday destination, have actually paid little
attention to the speed with which we seem intent on destroying not
only our own castle culture but the other cultures of the world as
well.

Ruth Benedict did spend a good deal of time attempting to
achieve a comparative sociology, a means of defining what was
essentially her intuitive grasp of a basic distinction between cultures. Some, she felt, were anxious, surly, and full at once of low
morale and much hatred and aggression. Others were the opposite,
were calm, purposeful, and affectionate. Race, geography, climate, size, wealth provided no principles of classification; it was
only when she examined the function of behaviour that she found
the terms she desired: high synergy as opposed to low synergy.
These defined her secure and insecure cultures. Synergy is a
concept which has far from adequate dispersal, for it describes
much of the human success of the *tiers monde* while explaining a
good deal of the misery which is so seemingly inexplicable in the
castle culture: Harlem; the Gaspé; the three billion spent each year
on mental illness in America; what Radhakrishnan perhaps refers
to in his phrase "technological barbarism".

From her lengthy comparative studies Ruth Benedict concluded
that societies where non-aggression is conspicuous have social

orders in which *the individual by the same act and at the same time serves his own advantage and that of the group*. Among the Blackfoot Indians, for example, the "rich" man with a large herd and two cars is not even considered among the wealthy because of his denial of other members of the community. In societies of high social synergy their institutions ensure mutual advantages from their undertakings, while in societies of low social synergy the advantage of one individual becomes a victory over another, and the majority who are not victorious must shift as they can.

Abraham Maslow,[13] who has extended these ideas, partially through studies of the Northern Blackfoot Indians, notes other characteristics. High-synergy cultures have siphon systems of wealth distribution, such as ritual hospitality by the rich, co-operative techniques of food sharing, or, in modern times, graduated income taxes. Low-synergy societies have funnel mechanisms for wealth distribution, such as exorbitant rents, usurious interest, and greater taxation of the poor than of the rich. High-synergy societies emphasize the use of an object rather than its specific ownership, stress-comforting and beneficence through religion rather than wrath or vengeance, and have techniques developed for working off humiliation. In low-synergy societies, life is humiliating, embarrassing, and hurting.

Maslow is probably correct in asserting that if any Utopia is to be constructed it must have as one of its main foundations a set of high-synergy institutions. The racial slums, or hell-topias, of America obviously fulfil all the technical conditions of a low-synergy society: no mutual advantages from actions, funnel mechanisms for distribution of wealth, and lasting humiliations. Any colonial situation, whether in Quebec or South Africa, represents the imposition of low-synergy conditions upon the colonized, whose survival often depends upon the creation of illicit, high-synergy institutions, but whose freedom seldom arrives without the development of aggressive, violent, low-synergy movements such as Black Power or the *Front de Libération Québécois*.[14]

The libertarian, especially in Canada, is at sea when dealing with such realities. Just when violence seems nearly under control

because of the extremity of nuclear-fisted violence, those old yet
acceptable ideals of individual freedom and national self-
determination begin to bind themselves up with *plastiques* and
machine-guns and Mao's exhortations. Canada's deft pattern of
moving from colony of France to colony of England to colony of
America is ignored, in favour of the French/American/Irish/
Bolivian/Tanzanian patterns of wars of national liberation. And
neo-colonialism, or economic colonialism, is accepted as no better
a state than that of "pure" nineteenth-century colonialism by the
Guevaras and the Nkrumahs. The bewildered libertarian finds
violence presented as an alternative to grantings of dubious char-
ity.

Active Canadian reactions to the new worlds find their base either
in our heritage of Christian *caritas* or the obvious success of our
participation in castle science and technology. M.I.T. replaces the
cathedral. The External Aid Office now exports entire schools
based on the Ryerson Institute of Technology; Cardinal Léger
declares for deeds rather than words and heads for the starving
lepers in Africa. Canada Plus-One, with an initial donation of one
hundred thousand dollars from the Hustlers' Bible Class, launches
a million-dollar Food and Agricultural Organization drive to improve third-world methods of processing and distributing food.
Dagmar Langer declares for man deserving man, while the Wards
argue for a new jeep.

   For the Canadian activists in the third world, the Barbara Ward
position is generally accepted. Savings and science are the keys to
the revolution of economic growth, and the revolution of scientific
and capitalist change will hopefully decide the biological revolution as well. Families will decrease in size as social security
becomes a reality.[15]

   The hoped-for model is the Houphouët-Boigny or Ivory Coast
model, wherein the developing country asks for aid without em-
barrassment and yet without arrogance, confident of human sol-
idarity and brotherhood and doing everything necessary to merit
the confidence of the aiders and the investors.[16]

Yet even Houphouët-Boigny must question the widening gap between the increasing cost of industrial products and the decreasing value of agricultural products and raw materials.[17]

For there are, inevitably, many violent reactions to this modern version of Disraeli's Two Nations. Jean-Paul Sartre not only accepts Frantz Fanon's welcoming of violence but finds the castle nations totally involved in the process:

We too are being decolonized: that is to say that the settler which is in every one of us is being savagely rooted out. Let us look at ourselves, if we can bear to, and see what is becoming of us. First we must face that unexpected revelation, the strip-tease of our humanism. There you can see it, quite naked, and it's not a pretty sight. It was nothing but an ideology of lies, a perfect justification for pillage; its honeyed words, its affectation of sensibility were only alibis for our aggressions. A fine sight they are too, the believers in non-violence, saying that they are neither executioners nor victims. Very well, then; if you're not victims when the government which you've voted for, when the army in which your younger brothers are serving without hesitation or remorse have undertaken race murder, you are, without a shadow of a doubt, executioners. And if you choose to be victims and to risk being put in prison for a day or two, you are simply choosing to pull your irons out of the fire. But you will not be able to pull them out; they'll have to stay there until the end. Try to understand this at any rate: if violence began this very evening and if exploitation and oppression had never existed on the earth, perhaps the slogans of non-violence might end the quarrel. But if the whole regime, even your non-violent ideas, are conditioned by a thousand-year-old oppression, your passivity serves only to place you in the ranks of the oppressors.[18]

And such a position, inspired by the excesses of the Algerian war, finds strong support within China. And more support than we are perhaps willing to admit within America itself:

But finally all this material existence of the European will be burned. I mean that literally and symbolically. It will be burned in flames, you see? It is almost as if to provide heat and light for the new societies. So I always look at this society as *dead wood*, to be burned so as to provide new beings with heat and light.[19]

Against such an increasing polarity, the sanity of Nyerere's *Ujamaa*, a theory of a unique African synthesis of man and society, probably holds much appeal as an ideal that Canada can recognize. For it was not merely to give that Léger departed for Africa, but partly out of dismay at the trends of Canadian secularism and partly in awe of the African paradox of great joy in the midst of great misery, a joy expressed in ritual movement and song much richer than all our abundance.

Ujamaa attempts to create a society in which all contribute to the material wealth and not solely to their personal material accumulations; a national ethos which incorporates the African traditions of social obligation and of sharing. Rather than basing our own decisions on idealistic reason and the relatively fresh traditions of the last few centuries, we should examine such systems carefully in terms of functional success and see whether they have not something to teach us.

For the alternative of America as Rome, towards which we seem to be hemming and hawing, lacks all humanistic validity. It is not just Mao who sees the trend toward imperialism in America. J. William Fulbright, Senate Foreign Relations chairman for many years, has observed the political force of the massive military-industrial-university complex at a time when the foreign aid total is the smallest in twenty years, when a defence budget totals seventy-nine billion, with forty-five billion being poured into defence-oriented companies, and when defence spending supports more than ten per cent of the American labour force. "This may culminate in our becoming an empire of the traditional kind," he states, "ordained to rule for a time over an empty system of power and then to fall and fade, leaving, like our predecessors, a legacy of dust."[20]

But it will not be an empire of the traditional kind; that should be obvious. For what separates our century from all others is the constant burst and flowering of technological innovation, what Buckminster Fuller calls "more-with-lessing", or progressive ephemeralization. The American HES system is an example of how this innovation can be put to use within a given colony: computer cards are filled out for each hamlet and run through computers in Saigon and Bangkok; a Hamlet Evaluation System is thus created which proves that the "secure" population in South Vietnam has increased by more than a million since January.

All our recon information is filed cross-indexed in Tan Son Nbut. . . .
  Recon also keeps a running check of where our own troops and the Arvins are . . . (it is considered bad for morale to drop bombs on your own guys). The men in the read-out rooms at Tan Son Nbut look like space-laboratory technicians. They wear white skull caps and long gauntleted white gloves to keep dandruff and sweat marks off delicate material. Be a shame to call a bomb strike on a bit of dandruff, or interpret a sweat mark as a VC trench.[21]

  It is not my purpose to investigate the particular horror of the American "presence" in Vietnam. Those who believe in the ideal of the independence of nations have their own opinions of the American contribution to the Western gas-chamber tradition — that combination of polystyrene, benzine, and gasoline known as napalm-B.
  As far as the individual is concerned, American militarism is not surprising. Militant enthusiasm in man is a true autonomous instinct with its own appetitive behaviour, its own releasing mechanisms, and its own specific feelings of intense satisfaction.[22] If "Canada First" again became an ideal, and groups of guerrillas were forced to destroy a factory of Litton industries, their motivations and pleasures would be exactly like those of a group of marines engaged in Operation Cedar Rapids. A similar "militancy" is observable in most peace groups.
  As far as the third-world nations are concerned, the only question is for what length of time they will be able to play the role that Martin Luther King played within the United States — of proving beyond a shadow of a doubt that any appeal to Christian virtue and pragmatic humility is going to earn nothing more than a pleasant liberal smile and a swift kick in the knackers.[23]

The technological horror of Vietnam will be repeated and repeated within our lifetimes. We must grapple with the general context, the source and the framework. When MacNamara is finished at the World Bank will he return to Ford or to the Defense Department or to Harvard University? What does George Grant mean by the continental state capitalist structure? Galbraith by a "technostructure"? If CUSO TWO is looking for a productive form, a structure of abundance, is there one at hand? Why should we not plan to use the extra-hands of technology, the megawatt slaves of science, to see the larger task accomplished.

For, paralleling the horrors that marked stages in the life of the CUSO "I" were inventions that perhaps saved his life, and certainly added to its pleasure. Salk's vaccine, the *Nautilus, Sputnik*, the discovery of the DNA genetic code, heart transplants, all these seemed to indicate that the great surge of free-willing energy kindled by the Enlightenment continued. In 1845, in the early years of Queen Victoria's reign, when Disraeli put into novelistic terms the conflict between the fox-hunting rich and the tenement poor, it was not possible even to consider expanding his sense of outrage from the world's major industrial nation to embrace the world itself. Now we can expand that sense of outrage. The present budget of the Province of Ontario would have shocked the financers of Disraeli's day. As B. Fuller points out, describing the "unflagging pregnancy" of modern invention:

It is inconceivable that one man, one party, one nation, or even a world congress of all mankind's representatives meeting a century ago (1865) — when a million dollars was an almost incredible sum, could have had the vision, logic, and courage to elect to invest 5 trillion dollars in the invention and development of the then uninvented and economically unanticipated telephone; electric light; radio; airplane; jet and rocket flight; nuclear reactor; flight into space; world-around television; elimination of both bacterial and virus diseases; discovery and isolation of 60 additional chemical elements and their electrons and nuclear components; and the genetic code; together with 10 million additional, mutually

inter-advantaging, technical inventions and discoveries which have occurred in the last century; plus development of industrial mass-
production and its progressive industrial-production-capacity-geared-
accrediting of the paper-financed, mass-consumption industry; tripling
of human longevity and the support of three times as many people on
earth, half of them at standards of living better than any king has ever
known.

During the first half century of the airplane, the major sovereign
powers poured $2^1/2$ trillion dollars directly and indirectly into aircraft
development as the new supreme weapon. Now in one-third that time the
world nations have again appropriated almost as much capability wealth
for the development of the atomic-headed rocketry and space race, for
supreme control of the earth and its surrounding portion of the universe.[24]

If anyone considers the political effect of the mere longbow and
the pike as new weapons in the Middle Ages, it would perhaps
hardly be exaggeration to suggest that the forms of human organization such an exploding galaxy demands would differ slightly
from those rigid nineteenth-century forms from which politicians
derive their ideological vigour and aggressive slogans.

As historically befits the self-conscious colony, the Ontario
heartland, that true focus of most non-reactionary thought in
Canada, has produced (if not always retained) a large number of
commentators upon this new industrial system: McLuhan, Grant,
Innis, Galbraith.

What Galbraith has now very clearly documented is that modern
large corporations and the modern apparatus of socialist planning
are variant accommodations to the same need. The inadequacy of
old democratic socialism is the inadequacy of the old individual
capitalist.

The interference of a parliament, then, is no less disruptive than
the interference of an owner-entrepreneur — when the productive
structure reaches the necessary size of an Air India or a General
Motors. For step by step with this growth of inter-advantaging
invention and knowledge has come a revolution of formal organization: the shift from land-power to capital-power has been followed by a shift from capital-power to managerial-power.

The multiplicity, or dynamic fragmentation, and specialization which Henry Adams examined in his 1907 autobiography was increased by the invention-impetus of the two world wars (however destructive), and in the postwar period has reached a point where what may be crudely termed the "composite brain" is necessary for the majority of man's enterprises.[25]

Galbraith's word for this is the technostructure, that circle of technicians, engineers, sales executives, scientists, designers, and other specialists, who contribute to those group decisions which mark the guiding intelligence of the enterprise and which the management has no successful option but to follow.

The more thorough-going the application of the sophisticated technology, the more inevitable and complex the function of this technostructure. Immense amounts of time and capital must be applied; this application creates its own inflexible demands; specialized skills in production and marketing require a corresponding specialization in co-ordination; the extent of this interacting and massively financed matrix eventually makes a lack of extensive planning suicidal.

The corporation is obviously far from suicidal in nature. The corporation succeeds by its autonomy. It generates its own capital. It trusts its technostructure.

Of the one hundred and eight billion dollars saved for investment in America in 1965, more than eighty-three billion was saved by corporations. Few would deny, however strongly anti-de Gaulle, that the ability to direct this flow of savings represents considerable power, especially when it is a few hundred corporations which provide the bulk of such direction.

To retain this autonomy, the technostructure must make use of the myth of consumer control of the market. Demand cannot be managed without the greatest possible freedom in the exercise of persuasion. So rather than admit its strength, admit its control of market and manipulation of demand — which are not necessarily evils in the age of abundance — the technostructure bows in mock fealty to the all-powerful Mr. Consumer who has just overthrown General Motors by refusing to buy his biennial Pontiac.

Planning equals communism, say the Arizona priests, but although it utilizes the myth for self-preservation the state capitalist structure in reality is far from agreement. The system utilizes government as a balancing act, to ensure that savings are used and that investment and consumption are limited to savings. In weaponry, space exploration, transport planes, and applied nuclear energy, it utilizes government contracts to replace market uncertainty with assured prices and profits. General Dynamics, Boeing, and Lockheed all sell more than sixty-five per cent of their production to the government; Canadian Bell and most of our pipelines accept a government-regulated profit-limit as part of the price of size and monopoly. And, as the size of the trade unions decreases, that of the educational establishment increases with the full blessing and assistance of the state,[26] for the workers are on the outer rings of this structure and the men near the centre have all the initials after their names. A BSC is only a squire; the PHD is a knight. One need only examine the calendar of York University, state- and industry-blessed, to see the process in great detail.

When Irving Layton, ex-Jewish intellectual, ex-Marxist, ex-poetic humanitarian, describes his support of Johnson and the Vietnam war as true prophecy, the force of economic fact buttresses him. "A poet knows what the *Zeitgeist* is labouring to produce."

Canada is probably the first, although France is quickly becoming more vocal[27] in her protests, to feel the brunt of this shift from capital-power to managerial-power. As Grant has clearly indicated,[28] the primary purpose in Canadian society is to keep technology dynamic within the context of the continental state capitalist structure. After the failure of the system to produce savings during the thirties and the debacle of World War Two, it perhaps seemed justifiable to the Howe-men to sell Canada piecemeal to those technostructures, predominantly American, who knew how to produce, how to generate savings internally, how to manipulate demand, and how to supersede the market amongst themselves whenever necessary. The minute percentages of our oil, chemical, automobile, and manufacturing industries owned by ourselves is a statistic known by us all and is a mark of fiefdom we manage to keep quite well hidden beneath our one-hundred-and-fifteen-dollar British suits and our ten-dollar Italian ties.

Even the Irish would find it difficult to stir up revolution against a Shell production team or an IBM computer systems-group. The student from a developing nation might do well to examine the past twenty years of Canadian history as an object lesson in the painless transition from dubious nation to gutless, if affluent, satellite.

But there is one further fact which we can isolate by defying McLuhan a moment longer and checking our rear-view mirror. The crux of technology as religion is that it is supposedly value-free; ideas of human excellence are seen as vestiges of religious and metaphysical superstitions which still bar the liberty of the individual. Yet the prime value of the technostructure, the pursuit of technological efficiency to increase consumption or the GNP, is accepted with only microscopic scepticism or complaint by the public realm as the proper and unquestioned value/goal of the society.[29]

CUSO must be seen within this context and the developing nations (including Canada) must be aware of its implications.

Although a certain amount of his personal motivation may come from the value-lack of his own society, the CUSO volunteer is so seldom rejected abroad precisely because he is so indeterminate about what human excellence consists of, beyond his acceptable acknowledgement of the value of an increasing GNP for Zambia or Jamaica or Ceylon or wherever.[30]

As long as the combination of Marines, Special Forces, affluence over-spill, and futile UN sanctions can contain and defuse the peasant-city wars in which Mao still naively trusts, Layton is a true prophet; the development of this American-based state capitalist structure is the certain wave of the future. As trade followed the flag, the state industrial system will follow (where it, likewise, has not already preceded) the volunteer.

Certainly a mixed blessing, I will agree. As in Justinian's reconquering of the Western Empire, or ancient Rome's ''pacification" of Britain, one is reminded of Tacitus' epigram: "They made it a desert and called it peace."

But if one turns now to the future, it must be forgotten that the "unflagging pregnancy" of inventiveness has not yet gobbled its own pill or accepted its own plastic ring. Much of the affluence of the North American continent is based on the low proportion of the labour force (eight to twelve per cent) diverted to the production of the nation's sustenance. Inventiveness and technology have been successful with little real difficulty and the potential for even greater reduction of the labour/yield ratio is present.

This is the crux. Combine, somehow, inventiveness and vast amounts of cheap energy and the individual's desire to create social change and to share cultures, combine these somehow, find a structure of abundance, and our castle security and fertility might become as common as Okanagan Valley apples. This entire book has dealt with the force of individual desire to learn and to serve; the necessary discoveries are of the present not the future. Here are six recent miracles.

The Rosner Chair at the University of Manitoba has made possible the first fertile crossbreed of grain ever accomplished by man. This high-yield crossbreed of wheat and rye, triticale, without special equipment or management, can produce a yield of twenty-five to forty per cent more than traditional crops. The Rockefeller-backed Mexican variety of wheat, short-stemmed and rust-resistant, is already producing amazing crops and by 1971 India hopes to have ten per cent of all her grain lands under these new high-yield varieties of wheat and rice.

Caloric deficiencies are a better known, but no more destructive, factor in the poverty cycle than protein deficiencies. Infant mortality, poor resistance to disease, inferior mental development, and lowered vigour are all documented results of protein lack.[31] The amino-acid pattern of proteins of milk and eggs can be approached in the pattern for cereal proteins by the addition of lysine; or protein quality of cereals can be improved by the addition of protein concentrates such as those from soy or fish.[32] Indeed,

Purdue's new *opaque-2* corn itself contains up to one hundred per cent more lysine than normal hybrid corn and in tests in Guatemala has been shown to have the protein quality of milk.[33] At a cost of less than one-half cent per day, the diets of many undernourished people could be balanced by the addition of fish protein concentrate, produced by a method already validated.

More experimentally, but perhaps eventually more efficiently, the USSR, Esso, and BP have reached the semi-industrial stage in a method of producing protein yeasts from petroleum fermentation.[34] In the light of present knowledge, the potential tonnage of proteins thus derived may be estimated at nearly twenty million tons per annum — while the estimated additional production of proteins needed by 1980 will reach only seventeen million tons.

And most experimental, yet as promising, are the technical and economic feasibility studies done by the Oak Ridge National Laboratory on atom farms, or what they awkwardly term Nuclear-Powered Agro-Industrial Complexes.[35] One of these would take an arid, potentially fertile desert near the sea as its base. To feed a million people would require one hundred and eighty million gallons a day, a twenty-two-hundred-megawatts reactor, and an irrigated area ten miles square. Effectively, a technostructure would run the entire area as a factory-farm. Fertilizer would be produced on the site, using power from the reactor. The distilled water would be delivered under pressure in closed pipes. Seed used would be tested and controlled. A central laboratory would analyse soils and determine fertilizer mix. Nearly continuous production would be ensured through careful rotation and the benefits of a constant sun. At various levels of technology, the cost per day per person fed by such a farm would descend from a currently possible 4.5 cents to a probable 1.8 cents.

Let us ignore the possibilities of adding manufacturing complexes to such a basic unit. Let us ignore the development of truly low-cost energy through the advanced breeder-reactor, whereby many industrial processes would be transformed by the substitution of cheap energy for raw materials such as coke, natural gas, or high quality ores. We must still admit that it is here that the doomsday idealist might find firm ground for a regrouping of his forces. It is with such energy-multipliers that he might conquer the sense of futility which comes to him on the Ganges Plain or when leaving Upper Volta. To work out these possibilities is an alternative to Vietnamism.

The famines and wars which face us, which we help create by neglect or by possessive greed, are as conquerable as TB and malaria. We need only, and I say this without qualification, make the decision to act. It is within the economic capability of the castle nations, as it is within their technological capability, to build not one but a dozen of these Atom Farms within the next five years. All that is in question is our humanistic will to action. The Atom Farm is the most dramatic innovation; the more mundane discoveries are still bold enough. We need only to decide to act.

Far be it from me to ignore my earlier conclusion and pretend that such a decision would not have to be made by a "composite-brain", but if I were to say that after learning and serving must come innovation, if I were to imagine a second-generation CUSO, which from time to time I do, it would have to follow these lines:

a) Be as high-synergistic as the present CUSO in terms of identification, *caritas*, and *Ujimaa*;

b) Admit that individualism is essentially a virtue of the past and put together an international technostructure capable of accomplishing some major task or series of tasks chosen by group decision;

c) Acknowledge the efficiency and potential high synergy (if given values) of the modern corporation and attempt to work with one or a number of these in the accomplishment of the task(s), as well as with host nationals and the Canadian government;

d) Not be afraid to borrow and manage and regenerate capital for the accomplishment of the task;

e) Be prepared for those outbreaks of intra-specific aggressive behaviour which could doom the entire project.

I do not pretend that this CUSO TWO would restore our nation's sense of identity, enable us to repurchase our oil fields, make the entire world as happy and contented as our Cree-Canadians, and/or prevent the Damocletian sword from falling. That the concept is a practical possibility, however, says a great deal about the nature of our world. There is no reason why we should not add to the stockpile of our visions the specific vision of wiping out poverty and hunger in, let us say, all of East Africa.

One could, alternatively, agree with Heidegger that for the castle nations the entire past twenty-five hundred years have been but a single epoch. And that this epoch has been marked by that objectification of Being whose final master is the force of technology. And that the philosophic possibilities of the era are exhausted, without changes in the total outlook of man, though the possibilities *in detail* of science and technology remain without limit.

Yet still, while we wait for the long night that must precede new dawns of philosophy, one could do worse than identify with such a CUSO TWO. Then, at least, one would be elephant against elephant, and not one in a mere succession of Whipper Billy Watson gnats. Man *deserves* man, and on our present course that is exactly what he will receive: such crowding of territories as can only result in war and famine. Man *requires* something more than man, some structure within our single technological world that can batter and destroy the problems rather than eradicate man himself. The chances of this arriving are somewhat slimmer than the chances for famine and the sword. The need for this arriving is the great need of our time.

DAVID SUZUKI

Genetics: Will This Science Save Us or Kill Us?

IN THE PAST 20 years, the science of "molecular genetics" has dazzled the world with its insights into living organisms. What is genetics? Genetics is a science which tries to understand how characteristics are passed from parent to child — how did you get your mother's smile or your father's temper? We know that we start life as a single cell when an egg is fertilized by a sperm.

Contained in that tiny amount of protoplasm there must be a blueprint from a mother and father which tells that cell how to make a complex animal called a person who is made up of 60 *trillion* cells. How? That is the challenge for genetics.

Remarkably, geneticists find that all organisms — viruses, elephants, carrots, and people — obey the same basic laws of inheritance. So studies on heredity (the transmission from parent to offspring of certain characteristics) in fruit flies or corn plants can tell us things about ourselves. Already, genetics has been applied with considerable effect on society. We don't even think about breeds of dogs, giant flowers, or seedless watermelons.

In economic terms, millions of dollars have been made by development of rapidly maturing, disease-resistant plants, high-yield rice, hybrid corn, moulds with high anti-biotic yields, and special breeds of cattle, hogs, and chickens. Some inherited diseases and defects in man can now be diagnosed and corrected or prevented.

In the past 20 years, it has been shown that the inherited blueprint that determines the shape of our noses, colour of eyes and hair, etc., actually is a chemical substance or molecule commonly called DNA (deoxyribonucleic acid). Molecular geneticists showed that genetic information is written much like code on a ticker tape. The biological language has four letters which are molecules with specific shapes and are hooked together like beads on a string in DNA.

DNA can have millions of these letters linked together. The words in the biological dictionary are all uniformly three letters long. With a four-letter alphabet, there are 64 different three-letter words or triplets. A sentence is written out by stringing together several hundred triplets.

Since one DNA molecule can have many sentences, one of the triplets is used as a capital letter designating ''start reading here'' and three triplets act as either commas or periods that signal ''end of message''. These sentences are called *genes* and it is known that viruses may have six to 100 genes; bacteria, a few thousand; and fruit flies, 100,000. Each cell in a human being carries the equivalent of 1,000 volumes of the complete works of Shakespeare; that's how much information is required for that egg to make a person.

The way cells read genes and translate them into the countless number of chemical events occurring within cells is now known and represents an immense leap in our understanding of life. Virus genes which can infect living cells have been replicated in test tubes. Indeed, starting with the four letters of the genetic alphabet, chemists have joined them together to make complete sentences and now propose to package these man-made genes into viruses which will inject them into cells. This holds the hope of curing inherited diseases by introducing good man-made genes into people with the disease.

Returning to the 1,000-volume blueprint in a fertilized human egg, we can ask: How is the information used to make muscle, bone, and skin cells? It is now clear that specific signals direct different cells to read certain chapters in the blueprint (i.e., a cell is told "read those chapters for making nuscle" and thus becomes a muscle cell). If all cells in our bodies have the entire blueprint, then it should be possible to trick a skin cell, for example, to read back at the beginning and make a complete person who is identical to the skin donor. This is exactly what English novelist Aldous Huxley (1894–1963) predicted in *Brave New World* and has already been accomplished with plants and frogs and appears imminent with mice. This holds the potential for making thousands of genetically identical people.

Another possibility arises from knowing that development and differentiation occur by selected readings of the genetic blueprint. When a finger is amputated, if the cells around the cut could read the right chapters, it should be able to grow another finger. This has already been done in frogs and may be possible with mice and man in our lifetime.

Historically, Canada has had excellent people in agricultural and human genetics. The breeding of rapidly maturing strains of wheat at the Central Experimental Farms in Ottawa permitted crops to be grown in short prairie seasons. The University of Alberta has an excellent program in the breeding of cattle and hogs. Research is now extending to the genetics of fish and forest trees and to the use of mutations (sudden variations in inheritable characteristics) for pest control.

Dr. Howard Newcombe at Chalk River pioneered large-scale computer analysis of genes in Canadian populations. Many people have analyzed the inheritance of human diseases as Mongolism (a type of mental deficiency certain people are born with) and cleft palate. Scientists led by Dr. Louis Siminovitch at the University of Toronto are studying methods of testing for inherited defects in an early embryo in the mother's body. Already, there is a special technique which permits doctors to determine whether a mother who had German measles (rubella) may have a defective child or whether a child will have Mongolism or Rh difficulties. Incidentally, this technique also permits doctors to determine the sex of a child.

As with all scientific discoveries, the application of genetic knowledge can be used for the benefit or detriment of society, and decisions for its use require considerable foresight and wisdom. Techniques permitting the detection and prevention or correction of inherited defects can help to eliminate suffering and expense to society and afflicted individuals. But who will make the decisions — the pregnant woman, doctors, members of Parliament? What risks of a defect will be accepted? What will be decided against— diabetes, short-sightedness, albinism, harelip? There is no question in my mind that society can benefit greatly from foetal analysis (analyzing unborn young) and abortion of genetic defects. If the present trend towards restriction of family size continues, pregnancy will be a more serious condition that we will want to ensure will result in a healthy child.

However, we are still haunted by the spectre of Hitler's infamous pseudogenetic extermination of Jews to produce a superior race. There is no shortage of superstitions, old wives' tales, and just plain prejudice which could be used to justify discriminatory biological programs. The most recent example was the statement by the newly elected President of the Canadian Medical Association. He suggested that educated, higher-income groups are restricting family size and therefore being outbred by lower-class groups, and that recipients of welfare should be sterilized.

It is highly questionable whether social position has a genetic basis or that upper-class people have greater wisdom or better human qualities. Others suggest that greater intelligence is highly desirable and should be selected for by incentives for college graduates to have lots of children. Again, as a university teacher, I find it hard to believe that a college degree is a good indicator of intellectual ability or that it indicates a "better" person. I doubt that we have sufficient knowledge or wisdom to apply genetics to man on a large scale.

The promise of molecular genetics is its ultimate application for the correction of diseases such as diabetes, sickle cell anemia, mental retardation, etc., possibly by the introduction of good, man-made genes. Indeed, some scientists in the U.S. have introduced a bacterial gene picked up by a virus into human cells in tissue culture and "cured" the disease.

However, we are again faced with the realization that defective genes could also be used as a weapon to *induce* defects in normal people. Perhaps the most horrendous example of the terrible inventiveness of scientists and the military is a paper in the December, 1970, issue of *Military Review* entitled "Ethnic Weapons". Dr. Carl Larson, a geneticist in Sweden, pointed out racial differences in susceptibility to a number of chemicals. He suggests, therefore, that weapons which kill specific racial groups could be constructed. It seems to me that one way of reducing the chance of such misuse of science is through a public informed about science and fully aware of its potential use.

One argument often made is that medicine allows many genetically defective people to survive and even to breed. Consequently, so the argument goes, more bad genes are passed on and the population becomes "weaker". Let us examine this position. Most genetic defects are caused by *recessive* genes; that is, in order to have the disease, one has to have two defective genes, one from each parent. If one has a good and a bad gene (such people are called "carriers"), a person is normal but will pass the bad gene on to half of his children. For every defective person, there will be many normal carriers.

Let us consider a recessive disease, phenylketonuria (PKU) which results in extreme mental retardation and occurs about once in every 10,000 births in Canada. PKU can be diagnosed at birth and appears to be correctable by special diets. If all PKUs were detected, cured, and had children, it would take over 1200 years to *double* the number from 1 to 2 in 10,000. That's hardly a staggering increase in our genetic burden.

The potential for genetics for the benefit of mankind is already being realized in the so-called Green Revolution. Canada stands to benefit economically and in quality products through plant and animal breeding programs. Moreover, the potential control over many inherited defects will relieve much personal unhappiness and cost.

However, we must be constantly aware of possible mischief that could result from the misuse of the same knowledge. The most successful species maintain a great deal of genetic diversity and we must not lead man into a blind alley by attempting to direct his evolution along a narrow channel. We are accumulating knowledge which permits us to tamper with the essence of man's nature through his genes, but we must have the wisdom to recognize our ignorance of the ultimate consequences of our actions.

Biographical Notes

Pierre Francis de Marigny Berton was born in Whitehorse, Yukon, in 1920, and educated in British Columbia. He now lives in Kleinburg, Ontario. His career as a journalist and editor took him from Vancouver, where he worked for the *News Herald* and the *Sun*, to Toronto, where he worked variously with the *Star*, *Maclean's*, and the Canadian Broadcasting Corporation, becoming a television personality, a best-selling author, and a director of McClelland & Stewart. His several books include *Klondike* (1958), *The Comfortable Pew* (1965), *The National Dream* (1970), and *The Last Spike* (1971). "On Racial Origins" is taken from *Just Add Water and Stir* (1959).

Alan Brown, now director of Radio Canada International in Montreal, has worked for the CBC as a producer, as the manager of Canadian Armed Forces radio stations in Europe from 1958 to 1967, and as English-language Radio Programme Director from 1967 to 1970. Born near Peterborough, Ontario, in 1920, he was educated at the University of Toronto, and is fluent in several languages. He has a well-established reputation as a translator of French and of French writers; among the works he has translated are Jacques Godbout's *Salut Galarneau!*, Hubert Aquin's *L'Antiphonaire*, and Naim Kattan's *Le Réel et le théâtral*.

Donald Allan Cameron, born in Toronto in 1937, grew up in Vancouver and was educated in British Columbia, California, and London. After a brief academic career in Vancouver and Halifax, he became a prolific freelance writer, making his home in Descousse, Nova Scotia. He was a founder of the magazine *The Mysterious East*, and has won a substantial reputation as a critic (*Faces of Leacock*, 1967), as an interviewer (*Conversations with Canadian Novelists*, 1973), and, in his many stories and articles, as a cultural commentator.

H. Northrop Frye is a professor of English at Victoria College, University of Toronto. Born in Sherbrooke, P.Q., in 1912, and educated at Toronto and Oxford in divinity and literature, he became one of the world's most influential literary critics and a specialist in myth criticism. He has published essays in a wide variety of journals, and among his books are *Fearful Symmetry* (1947), *Anatomy of Criticism* (1957), *The Modern Century* (1967), and *The Bush Garden* (1971). "The Motive for Metaphor" is the first of a series of six radio talks he delivered over the CBC in 1962 as the second series of the Massey Lectures; they were collected and published as *The Educated Imagination* in 1963.

Mavis de Trafford Gallant is a novelist and short-story writer who has lived in Europe since 1950 and is now resident in France. Born in Montreal in 1922, she was educated there, and was a film critic early in the 1940s. Since moving to Europe she has been a regular contributor to the *New Yorker*; "When We Were Nearly Young" and a number of her short stories first appeared in that magazine. Her writings include *My Heart Is Broken* (1959), *The Pegnitz Junction* (1973), *The End of the World and Other Stories* (1974), and a long introduction to *The Affair of Gabrielle Russier* (1971).

William David Godfrey has been called the most important Canadian fiction writer of his generation. A book of short stories, *Death Goes Better with Coca Cola* (1968), and a prize-winning novel called *The New Ancestors* (1970) both illustrate his cultural nationalism and his interest in the anthropological theories of Ruth Benedict, Margaret Mead, and Abraham Maslow. Born in 1938 in Winnipeg, he was educated in Canada and the United States; he has played in a jazz band, taught at Adisadel College (Cape Coast,

Ghana) and at the University of Toronto, and founded three independent publishing houses: Anansi, New Press, and Porcépic. "Doomsday Idealism" is from *Man Deserves Man* (1968), a series of essays by former CUSO workers, which he edited with Bill McWhinney.

George Parkin Grant comes from a family that included prominent nineteenth-century Canadian philosophers and theologians, and in his own work he has combined interests in philosophy and history with Christian belief. Born in 1918 in Toronto, he was educated there. In 1961 he became chairman of the Department of Religion at McMaster University in Hamilton, and he has been acclaimed as one of the most important intellectual essayists of modern Canada. His works have been particularly influential upon the Ontario novelists and poets of the 1970s, a group that includes Dave Godfrey, Dennis Lee, and Margaret Atwood; they include *Philosophy in the Mass Age* (1959), *Lament for a Nation* (1965), and *Technology and Empire* (1969).

Roderick Langmere Haig-Brown was born in Sussex, England, in 1908, emigrated to Canada in 1926, and was educated in both countries. He now lives in Campbell River, B.C., where for many years he was a judge of the Provincial Court. A noted conservationist, he has been a member of several international commissions, including the International Pacific Salmon Commission, and he has written widely on ecological subjects. *The Living Land* appeared in 1961, and his several reflective books on the art and action of fishing appeared during the 1950s and 1960s; "The Nature of Estuaries" is from *Fisherman's Fall* (1964). One of his books for children, *Saltwater Summer*, won a Governor General's Award in 1948.

Naim Kattan was born in 1928 in Baghdad, Iraq, and educated there and at the Sorbonne in Paris; he emigrated to Canada in 1954. He has been a literary critic for *Le Devoir* in Montreal and is currently head of the Literature and Publications Service of the Canada Council in Ottawa. Author of several plays and stories, he has also written a number of essays in both French and Arabic. He has been concerned with contrasting the intellectual perspectives of the Orient and the West, and with examining the impact of those differences both on the translation of ideas and languages and on the movement of people from one place to another. His work *Le Réel et le théâtral* won the France—Canada Prize when it first appeared in 1970; "The Word and the Place" is the concluding essay in it. The book was translated by Alan Brown in 1972.

Stephen Butler Leacock (1869—1944) emigrated with his parents from Hampshire to Canada when he was a small child. He grew up in rural Ontario — Orillia became the "Mariposa" of *Sunshine Sketches of a Little Town* (1912) — and received his university education in Toronto and Chicago. He became an economist and political scientist, influenced by the theories of Adam Shortt and Thorstein Veblen; he lectured in these disciplines at McGill University from 1903 to 1936, and he published a number of academic works. His international fame derived from his skill as a writer of humorous essays and anecdotes, and (in the Dickensian tradition) as a public reader of his own works. Within Canada, moreover, he has become something of a national institution. Along with *Sunshine Sketches*, his most memorable works include *Literary Lapses* (1910), *Arcadian Adventures with the Idle Rich* (1914), *My Discovery of England* (1922), and *My Remarkable Uncle* (1942).

John Hugh MacLennan is a novelist and professor of English at McGill University, and lives in North Hatley, P.Q. He was born in Glace Bay, Nova Scotia, in 1907, and educated in Classics at Dalhousie, Oxford (on a Rhodes Scholarship), and Princeton universities. His several novels, including *Barometer Rising* (1941), *Two Solitudes* (1945), and *Return of the Sphinx* (1967), have attempted to depict the psychological character and social structure of Canada; they are imbued with MacLennan's classical training, his sense of history, and his Cape Breton Presbyterianism. In his non-fiction—*Rivers of Canada* (1974), for example —he has also been concerned with charting the flow of history and demonstrating the distinctiveness of the Canadian experience. "By Their Foods . . . " is taken from *Scotchman's Return and Other Essays* (1960).

Fredelle Bruser Maynard grew up in the only Jewish family in a small prairie town. Her memoir of her childhood experiences is called *Raisins and Almonds* (1972); "The Windless World" is taken from this book. Her later education (at the universities of Manitoba, Toronto, and Harvard) took her to New England, where she has taught creative writing and written for a number of magazines. She now divides her time between New Hampshire and Toronto. An authority in child development and family life, she is also the author of *Guiding Your Child to a More Creative Life* (1973).

Peter Charles Newman was born in Vienna in 1929, emigrated in 1940, and was educated in Toronto, where he now lives. He has held several positions as a journalist: with the *Financial Post*, with the Toronto *Star*, and with *Maclean's*, which he has edited since 1971. He has also had a successful career as a television documentary scriptwriter. He is perhaps best known as a forthright political commentator, whose books — like *Flame of Power* (1959) and *Renegade in Power: The Diefenbaker Years* (1963)—analysed the power structures and political attitudes which governed Canada during the decades following the Second World War. The essays which make up "Czechoslovakia" were first published at various times in 1968 and 1970; they were collected in the form in which they are reprinted here in *Home Country* (1973).

Wilder Graves Penfield (1891-1976) was born in Spokane, Washington, and became a Canadian citizen in 1934, the year in which he took on the directorship of the Montreal Neurological Institute. He held that position until 1960, after which he became an Honorary Consultant there. A McGill professor of neurology, he earned much recognition for his research, and was the winner of a large number of medals and fellowships. In addition to his medical publications, he wrote two historical novels and several biographical, autobiographical, and reflective works, including *Second Thoughts: Science, the Arts and the Spirit* (1970), from which "The Superiority of the Bilingual Brain" is taken.

David Takayoshi Suzuki, born in Vancouver in 1936, was educated in the United States. He now teaches zoology at the University of British Columbia, and is a world-recognized expert in the study of genetics. Author of a large number of professional papers, he is also widely known for his lucid television programs on a variety of scientific subjects.

Frank H. Underhill (1889–1971), born in Stouffville, Ontario, and educated at Toronto and Oxford, became one of Canada's leading historians. A history professor at the universities of Saskatchewan and Toronto, and the Curator of Laurier House, Ottawa, he insisted on the need for academics to become actively involved in the political life of their society. He was one of the founding editors of the *Canadian Forum* in 1919, and was the author of the Regina Manifesto (the first party platform of the CCF). Several of his historical essays and political comments (including "Goldwin Smith") were collected in *In Search of Canadian Liberalism* (1960). *The Image of Confederation* appeared in 1964.

George Woodcock is Canada's leading "Man of Letters". Born in Winnipeg in 1912, he was educated in England and did not return to Canada until 1949; since then he has been a market gardener and a university lecturer, a poet, playwright, broadcaster, editor of *Canadian Literature*, and professional writer. His commitment to libertarian thought has led him not only to investigate anarchist and utopian ideas (as in *The Doukhobors*, with Ivan Avakumovic, in 1968) but also to eschew party politics, as illustrated in the essays (including "Encounter with an Archangel") collected in 1972 under the title *The Rejection of Politics and Other Essays*. A Vancouver resident, he is the author of many books of travel and social commentary (e.g., *Incas and Other Men*, 1959; *Faces of India*, 1964; *Canada and the Canadians*, 1969), several biographies (including one of his friend George Orwell, called *The Crystal Spirit*, 1966), critical writings (e.g., *Odysseus Ever Returning*, 1970), and histories (e.g., *Anarchism*, 1962, and *Who Killed the British Empire?*, 1974).

Footnotes

PENFIELD

1. In 1956, I delivered the Vanuxem Lectures at Princeton: "The Physical Basis of Speech", published later as *Speech and Brain Mechanisms*, Wilder Penfield and L. Roberts (Princeton: Princeton University Press, 1959). The last chapter turns to the subject of language learning. Chapters 12 and 13 of my more recent book, *The Second Career* (Boston and Toronto: Little, Brown and Company, 1963), also deal with second-language learning.

2. See Elizabeth Peel and W. E. Lambert, "The Relation of Bilingualism to Intelligence", *Psychological Monographs, General and Applied* (Washington, D.C.: American Psychological Association), Vol. LXXVI (1962), p.27, and W. E. Lambert and J. Macnamara, "Some Cognitive Consequences of Following a First-Grade Curriculum in a Second Language", *Journal of Educational Psychology*, Vol. LX (1969), pp.86-98.

3. Elizabeth Peel Anisfeld, *The Cognitive Aspects of Bilingualism* (Montreal: McGill University, PHD thesis).

4. E. G. Malherbe, *The Bilingual School* (London: Longmans, Green and Company, 1946).

KATTAN/BROWN

1. In the days of the Inquisition, Spanish Jews who were forced to become converts to Catholicism but continued to practise their own religion in secret were called by the Spaniards *marranos*, the hideous ones. (Tr.)

FRANK UNDERHILL

1. This article first appeared in the *University of Toronto Quarterly*, April 1933. I have tacked on to the end of it five paragraphs which formed the conclusion of a talk on Goldwin Smith that I gave over the CBC on December 6, 1950. Since my article appeared in 1933 two large-scale studies of Goldwin Smith have been done, one in the form of a Toronto PHD thesis by Ronald McEachern (unpublished), and the other a book by Elisabeth Wallace, *Goldwin Smith: Victorian Liberal* (Toronto: University of Toronto Press, 1957).

GRANT

1. In speaking of North American society, I do not wish to imply that there is no difference between Canada and the United States. I am a firm believer in the idea of British North America. But, for the present purposes, there is no need to make that distinction.
2. Such a statement is, of course, dependent on the supposition that the Roman Catholic Church will never take into itself the truth of freedom which Protestantism knows.

GODFREY

1. It will be a fundamental premise of this article that Canada has lost any genuine economic autonomy and is losing political independence at an accelerating pace.
2. One of numerous revealing statistics from John Laffin's perceptive *The Hunger to Come* (New York: Abelard-Schuman, 1971).
3. The Director of the Kearney Foundation of Soil Science of the University of California at Davis, Dr. Perry Stout, made these observations in 1967.
4. Philip Sporn, *Energy: Its Production, Conversion and Use in the Service of Man* (Elmsford, N.Y.: Pergamon Press, 1963).
5. The theory and figures of this solution, fiction writers being notoriously inadept at both, come from research sponsored by the U.S. Atomic Energy Commission: Gale Young's "Apollo Over the Ganges". An unpublished paper.
6. R. Buckminster Fuller, "Utopia or Oblivion", *Art Journal*, Vol. 6, 1967.
7. Over $370,000,000 of Canadian-made arms and military equipment, most of it destined for use in Vietnam, most of it produced by U.S. subsidiaries, went south in 1967.

8. P. G. Stafford and B. H. Golightly's *L.S.D.: The Problem-Solving Psychedelic* contains as good a bibliography as any (New York, N.Y.: Award Books, 1967).

9. For the influence of the Vietnam War on Canada's dollar, see Eliot Janeway's *The Economics of Crisis: War, Politics and the Dollar* (Toronto: Clarke, Irwin and Co., 1968). A complacency-blaster.

10. Those one or two who still believe in the home of the free might read for enlightenment Professor Stephen Rousseas' *The Death of a Democracy: Greece and the American Conscience* (New York, N.Y.: Grove Press, 1967).

11. If you consider John Calvin's theory of the total degradation of man invalid, try *Air War: Vietnam* by Frank Harvey. Copyright© 1966 by Ziff-Davis Publishing Company; Copyright© 1967 by Frank Harvey. Permission to reprint by Bantam Books, Inc.

12. Konrad Lorenz, *On Aggression*, trans. M. K. Wilson (New York, N.Y.: Harcourt Brace Jovanovich, 1966).

13. *Journal of Individual Psychology*, Vol. 20 (November 1964), pp. 153-164.

14. See Albert Memmi, *The Colonizer and the Colonized* (New York, N.Y.: Orion Press, Grossman, 1965); Major, *La Chair de Poule* (Parti Paris); Frantz Fanon, *Black Skin, White Masks*, trans. C. L. Markmann (New York, N.Y.: Grove Press, 1967).

15. Her "sustained and imaginative strategy of economic aid by the wealthy to the poor" has of course been farcically disproven by events during the Development Decade of the sixties. *The Rich Nations and the Poor Nations* (New York, N.Y.: Norton, 1962).

16. For example, the outline of his policies in *FAO Review*, Vol. 1, No. 1, January–February 1968.

17. Unreadable, but packed full of detail, is I. L. Horowitz's *Three Worlds of Development* (New York, N.Y.: Oxford University Press, 1966). Pages 164 to 192 especially deal with the ways in which the rich nations get richer (while feeling charitable) and the poor get poorer. Some fairly well-known summaries: Aid totals have remained static since 1961 at about $6 billion a year. Canada is increasing her GNP percentage, now 0.66% of national income, going to aid. Most other rich nations are cutting theirs. World U.S. aid is declining; fourteen days of the Vietnam war cost her as much as a year's aid. Service charges on public debt of recipient countries eat up almost two-thirds of the total aid given. Ken-

nedy Round tariff cuts *hurt* developing countries; their share of international trade has fallen from a third to a mere fifth in the past ten years.

18. Jean-Paul Sartre wrote the preface to Frantz Fanon's *The Wretched of the Earth*, one of the classics of our period. Translated from the French by Constance Farrington. Copyright© 1963 by *Présence Africaine* (New York, N.Y.: Grove Press, 1965).

19. LeRoi Jones. An interview with Austin Clarke.

20. For the full development of this argument, see *The Arrogance of Power* (New York, N.Y.: Random House, 1967).

21. Harvey, *Air War: Vietnam*.

22. Lorenz, *On Aggression*.

23. President Kenneth Kaunda of Zambia is only one "developing" leader who puts most of the "developed" to shame.

24. Written and copyrighted by Buckminster Fuller, 1965.

25. Although the effects have been known by writers for years, for theories and statistics of what follows I am indebted to Grant, *Lament for a Nation* (Toronto: McClelland & Stewart, 1965), and J. K. Galbraith, *The New Industrial State* (Boston: Houghton Mifflin, 1969).

26. The proposals for an International Development Centre in Canada illustrate this power of the educational establishment and its necessary relationship to government. Galbraith, Ward, and McLuhan have all been mentioned in association with this computer-focused academy, which would study world hunger, oceanic resources, multiracial societies, etc. The key mechanism of this "composite-brain" would be an information-retrieval system and data-processing equipment to coordinate and disperse the vast amounts of knowledge and invention available. Logical as it may be, it is still one of the most brilliant ideas ever to come out of Canada, and its side effects for corporational vitality and national identity could be enormous.

27. For the effects of this self-financing, computerized techno-structured corporationalism upon France, French book stores will provide Jean-Jacques Servan-Schreiber's *Le Défi Américain*.

28. George Grant's recent essays are soon to be collected. For the moment they may be examined within *The University Game* ("The University Curriculum"). Anansi Press.

29. "The fact that in our society the demands of technology are themselves the dominating morality is often obscured by the fact that the modern scientific movement has been intimately associated with the moral striving for equality." Grant in *The University Game*.

30. An enlightened self-interest is quite properly at work here. CUSO, in one sense part of the new social-innovation role of the university, finds a good deal of its support from the corporations that benefit from and direct the expansionary universities.

31. The classic work is A. M. Altschul's *Proteins: Their Chemistry and Politics* (New York, N.Y.: Basic Books, 1965).

32. Fish protein concentrates are already being produced industrially; shipments have been made to Korea. The Viobin Corporation was the pioneer. The U.S. Department of the Interior and even the Fisheries Research Board of Canada are at work. None of the following developments has as yet stirred up any Canadian interest, whether government or private.

33. Purdue University.

34. There is extensive, although primarily unpublished, literature on this development. See essentially reports of the World Petroleum Congress Panel 36, Mexico, 1967.

35. Again much of the literature is unpublished. The work of Alvin M. Weinberg, Gale Young, John W. Michel, and Philip Hammond of the Oak Ridge National Laboratory, Tennessee.